understanding
horses

An illustrated guide to a horse's behavior

understanding
horses

An illustrated guide to a horse's behavior

Don Harper

This is a Parragon Publishing book
This edition published in 2004

Parragon Publishing
Queen Street House
4 Queen Street
Bath BA1 1HE, UK

Copyright © Parragon 2001

ISBN 1–40540–734–4

Printed in China

Produced for Parragon by
The Bridgewater Book Company, UK

Editorial Director: Fiona Biggs
Art Director: Steve Wilson
Designer: Sarah Williams
Editorial Manager: Jane Laing
Editor: Jo Weeks

All pictures by
Bob Langrish except; p.12, The Ancient Art &
Architecture Collection Ltd; pp.14, 15, 30, Bruce
Coleman Collection; p.16 Bridgeman Art Library
(top) British Museum, London,
(bottom) Terme Museum, Rome, Italy

contents

introduction

Throughout the world today, horses still feature prominently in the lives of large numbers of people, just as they have done for thousands of years. But in the same way as our lives have changed over time, so has our relationship with the horse. From being essential on the battlefield and as a means of transportation, horses are now kept largely as companions and are often used for sporting purposes, ranging from horse racing to show jumping and polo to eventing.

Getting started

Even if you have never ridden before, it is generally easy to learn, with many reputable riding schools well established in numerous countries, teaching at all levels from novice to more advanced riding skills. You should, however, make sure that the school has a good reputation, with the instructors being suitably qualified in the area of riding that appeals to you. There is certainly no need or obligation to commit yourself to buying a horse at the outset, particularly since this will represent a substantial commitment – in terms of both finance and time. In addition, much of the equipment that you need can be borrowed or rented, although it is definitely a good idea to purchase your own riding helmet. This always needs to conform to the latest safety standards. One of the great things about riding on this basis is that you can go as frequently as your schedule permits, and it will generally work out much

cheaper than owing your own horse. Problems are more likely to crop up if you want to start competing, however, and this is the stage when you will need to consider obtaining your own horse, rather than using one regularly ridden by other people as well.

As a novice begins to ride more horses, so it soon becomes apparent that each mount differs in character, and these differences apply just as much to horses of the same breed as between breeds. Such temperamental variances depend partly on the past experience of each horse. There has been growing interest over recent years in the psychological makeup of horses and the way in which their natural behavior can influence their training, thanks partly to the popular book and film *The Horse Whisperer*. This interest has also led to a reappraisal of the best way to deal with horses suffering from behavioral problems, and experiments in novel ways of preventing them from arising in the first place. In turn, this has spawned developments such as stable toys, intended to keep horses from becoming bored in limited surroundings. Different treatments, often so-called alternative or complementary therapies such as acupuncture and Bach flower remedies, are also being used increasingly in the treatment of behavioral difficulties when they do arise in horses.

A number of these ideas, particularly relating to training, follow more intensive behavioral studies as to how horses behave naturally in herds, although there is actually no truly wild close relative of the domestic horse to be found in the world today. The last surviving species, Przewalski's horse (*Equus przewalski*), became extinct in the wild during the 20th century, but a well-coordinated captive breeding project has maintained its continued survival.

Riding and friendship

Although the plight of wild equids attracts relatively little attention today, the number of people who ride regularly continues to increase. For most people, being able to go out on a hack through the countryside is a truly relaxing experience, especially in countries such as the British Isles, where there is a well-established network of special bridleways, allowing you to ride in safety away from roads and enjoy splendid scenery as well. If you are feeling more competitive, however, there are many events and activities, ranging from dressage to cross-country jumping, in which you can participate.

Another of the pleasures of being involved with horses is that it can easily expand your circle of friends, especially if you have your horse stabled at a yard or simply ride regularly at the same school. Having horsey friends often makes keeping your own horse easier and might even help you to reduce the cost of various activities. For example, you may be able to find someone to share a trailer to a show or similar event, and when you cannot get to the stable, or when you want to take a vacation, someone will almost certainly be prepared to look after your horse, as long as you are happy to return the favor in due course.

Horses and vacations

Horses can become a passion, a fact that has not escaped the attention of some of the more specialized travel companies. If you fancy something different, you can go trekking among spectacular volcanoes in Iceland riding one of the hardy native Icelandic horses, or you might prefer to enjoy the spectacular landscape of the Welsh hills or the Rocky Mountains from the back of a horse. There is an ever-growing number of such options on offer. Before you go, be sure that you are fit enough to spend long days in the saddle, so you do not become unduly saddle sore, which could spoil your entire trip.

Should you be seeking a more leisurely break that includes horses, there are companies that will whisk you off to the awe-inspiring marshlands of the Camargue to track down the semi-wild gray horses that inhabit this unique area. Other options include tours to more formal settings in Austria, enabling you to gain insight into the famous Spanish Riding School of Vienna, including seeing the Lipizzaner stallions being put through their paces and visiting the stud farms.

You do not necessarily need to travel long distances to see horses at work, however. Even though they are no longer used routinely on farms, such is the current interest in working horses that they can be seen at many agricultural fairs and similar events, performing traditional tasks like plowing or pulling carts. In such situations, they invariably prove to be a major attraction for people of all ages.

a horse's basic nature

1 Although the tasks they perform for humans have changed since they were domesticated centuries ago, horses still play a significant role in the lives of many people. The story of equine evolution reveals just how lucky horses have been to survive to the present day. Their existence in North America, where much of their early evolution occurred, came to a dramatic end about 8,000 years ago, and they have been restored there only comparatively recently. Climatic changes also led to a reduction in their distribution in Eurasia, and, had it not been for domestication, they could have become extinct there, too. While domesticated horses have since thrived under human care, their wild relatives have not fared so well, many species having been hunted into oblivion in both Africa and Asia. The last extinction occurred in 1927, with the disappearance of the Syrian onager.

evolution
of the horse

Horse lineage can be traced back over 60 million years to a small creature called *Hyracotherium*, which stood about 8in (20cm) tall at the shoulder and measured 2ft (60cm) in length. *Hyracotherium* had a wide distribution; its remains have been unearthed in localities as far apart as North America, Europe, and Asia. Sixty million years ago, these areas were largely forested, and *Hyracotherium* browsed on low-growing plants, having 44 teeth with low crowns for this purpose (the modern horse has only 36). Its number of toes also exceeded those of today's horse, with four on each of the front feet and three on both of the hind ones.

Climatic changes that occurred during the Oligocene Period, about 38 million years ago, saw the *Hyracotherium* lineage vanish entirely from Eurasia, but its descendants flourished in North America. Here, the forests were gradually replaced by more open areas of country, and the lack of dense vegetative cover meant that speed became important as a means of defense against would-be predators: in order to survive, early horses were forced to start running. They also began to get bigger, and this is reflected in *Mesohippus*, which was more than twice the size of *Hyracotherium*.

Fewer toes and bigger teeth
Mesohippus had three toes on each foot, with the middle toe significantly longer than those on either side of it. Its head was longer as well, and its teeth also changed in shape, evolving a greater surface area for grinding purposes, although they were still set low in the jaw.

The development of high-crowned teeth confirms that from around this time horses began to switch from a browsing lifestyle to one that was based on grazing. This change becomes even more apparent in *Parahippus*, the successor to *Mesohippus*. The presence of hard silica in grasses, which had evolved by now, meant that its teeth would suffer heavy wear when grinding up this vegetation, in spite of the fact that they were additionally protected by a tough covering of cement.

Further development toward the modern horse can be seen in *Merychippus*, which followed *Parahippus*. Remains of herd members, dating back some 20 million years, have

The presence of horses in northern Europe led to them being portrayed in early cave art, which also reveals that they were initially hunted for food.

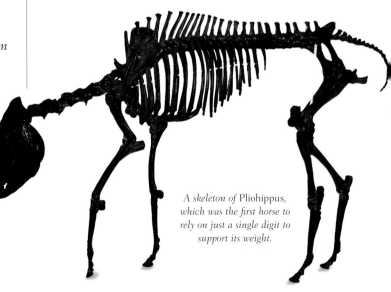

A skeleton of Pliohippus, *which was the first horse to rely on just a single digit to support its weight.*

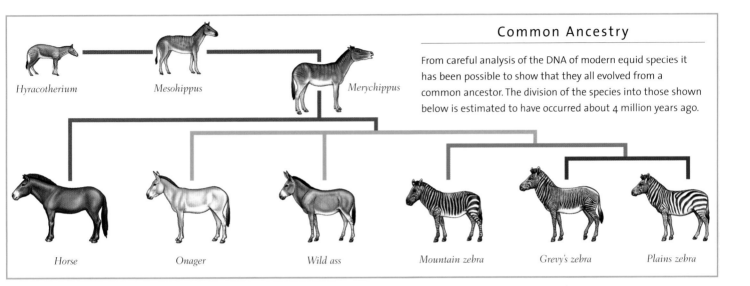

Common Ancestry

From careful analysis of the DNA of modern equid species it has been possible to show that they all evolved from a common ancestor. The division of the species into those shown below is estimated to have occurred about 4 million years ago.

Hyracotherium   *Mesohippus*   *Merychippus*

Horse   Onager   Wild ass   Mountain zebra   Grevy's zebra   Plains zebra

been found in grassland areas of Nebraska. The premolar teeth, located in front of the molars, also now had broader surfaces for grinding, and the jaw had become correspondingly heavier to accommodate them: it resembled that of a contemporary horse for the first time. In addition, the neck of *Merychippus* was longer, to facilitate its grazing lifestyle, allowing it to reach the ground easily. Changes in the foot structure also start to become apparent (see below). Only the central toe was now used for weight-bearing; the two side toes were smaller and were raised off the ground.

The development of the modern horse

Pliohippus was the first horse to have a foot structure like that of a modern horse, having just a single toe on each leg. This lineage continued to *Equus caballus*, which is considered to be the direct ancestor all today's equids. Its oldest remains, dating back over a million years, have been found in North America. At some point, earlier horse types had crossed the Bering land bridge back into Asia from North America, successfully colonizing this new land, and *Equus*, too, followed this route.

Members of the horse family also went westward and southward into Europe and Africa, but in North America itself, wild horses became extinct. Noone knows the reasons for certain, but the most likely explanation seems to be that an epidemic of a disease of some kind wiped them out. European colonists reintroduced horses to North America about 500 years ago.

The Evolution of the Hoof

The alterations in the structure of the horse's foot occurred partly as a result of changes in the environment. Having four toes like *Eohippus* was beneficial when it lived in marshy areas because it gave greater agility. Since then, the number of digits has dramatically reduced. But it is still possible to make out a trace of the horse's first digit, equivalent to our big toe, as the bony area above the knee and on the lower part of the hock joint, often known as the chestnut. The ergot, marking the fusion of the second and fourth digits, can be located at the back of the fetlock joints.

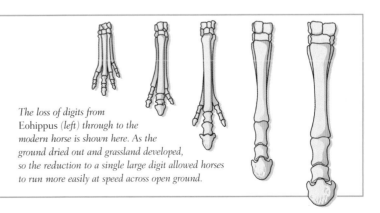

The loss of digits from Eohippus (left) through to the modern horse is shown here. As the ground dried out and grassland developed, so the reduction to a single large digit allowed horses to run more easily at speed across open ground.

zebras
and asses

There are now just six species of wild equid living in the world, with the distribution of the family being centered in Africa. This continent is home to the three species of zebra, as well as the African ass.

Grevy's zebra

Grevy's zebra lives in herds in arid areas in the far east of the African continent, in parts of Ethiopia, Somalia, and Kenya. Weighing about 900lb (405kg), it is the heaviest of all the wild horses.

The social structure in herds of Grevy's zebra, as well as those of wild asses, is very different to modern horses, with the bonds between members being much looser. This may be related in part to the fairly harsh habitat in which they live, since there is often not enough grazing to support large groups. Mature stallions establish fairly large territories, which can be up to 3.9 sq miles (10 square kilometers), marking the borders with dung to confirm their presence to others, and mating with mares that enter the region.

Plains zebra and mountain zebra

The lifestyle of the plains and mountain zebras differs from that of Grevy's, being more akin to that of true horses. These two species live in relatively stable herds, or harems, which consist of a stallion and several mares, and they occupy an established territory, known as their home range, which may be shared with neighboring harems. The plains zebra is found in grassland and savanna of East Africa, while the mountain zebra occurs at the other end of the continent, in the mountain grassland of the southwest.

Quagga

The Quagga was a very distinctive wild equid with a dark rump and stripes. Although originally considered to be a separate species, recent research suggests that it was a subspecies of the plains zebra, with stripes on just the head and upper part of the body. It was hunted to extinction in the late 1800s, but a breeding project is now underway to recreate this distinctive form.

Zebra Markings

The feature that sets zebras apart from the other members of this group is the striped patterning on their bodies. Grevy's zebra (*Equus grevyi*) has narrow black and white stripes that extend vertically up the sides of its body. The belly is white. Grevy's zebra also has a large, erect mane and unmistakable rounded ears. The plains or common zebra (*E. burchelli*) can be distinguished from Grevy's zebra by its much broader stripes, the lines curving to become more horizontal over the haunches. The mountain zebra (*E. zebra*) has stripes that are narrower and do not continue under the belly, which is white.

The presence of the distinctive stripes provides what is known as disruptive camouflage, helping to break up the outline of the zebra's body. This is especially beneficial when the zebras are close to each other in a herd, as it makes it harder for a would-be predator to pick out an individual.

Grevy's zebras: Amazing as it may seem, each zebra has an individual patterning.

Recent genetic research suggests that Przewalski's horse is not the direct ancestor of the domestic horse.

Tibet. Asiatic asses have much more rounded hooves, and they more closely resemble horses in terms of their overall appearance.

Przewalski's horse

The only wild horse in the world also occurs in Asia, found farther north than the Asiatic ass, in Mongolia. Przewalski's horse (*E. przewalskii*) inhabits open plains and semidesert areas in the vicinity of the Altai Mountains. This species first became known to western scientists in 1881. By the 1940s, it was considered to have become extinct in its native habitat, largely because of human pressures. But these tough and distinctive little horses have now been reintroduced to areas of their former range, and hopes are high that they will soon be thriving again in these surroundings.

African ass and Asian ass

The African ass (*E. africanus*) lives in the stony desert region of northeastern Africa, roaming through parts of the Sudan, as well as Ethiopia and Somalia. It is the smallest of all wild equids and has very narrow feet—an adaptation that helps it to walk easily as it is less vulnerable to foot injuries on the stony ground of its natural environment. The African asses' Asiatic counterpart (*E. hemionus*) ranges from Syria through parts of Iran and northern India to

The stripes of plains zebras extend around the underside of the body.

A mountain zebra: These particular zebras are now scarce in the wild.

domestication
of the horse

The ancestors of today's domesticated horses are thought to have originated from the plains of southern Russia, in the area between the Ukraine and Turkestan.

The domestication process is thought to have begun around 4000 B.C. At first, horses were probably kept for their meat and milk, but it was not long before they were being used to pull loads as well as being ridden. In the military arena, horses were originally kept for pulling chariots, and then they were used for cavalry purposes. For many centuries, they were ridden without stirrups. In fact, the earliest reference to stirrups is A.D. 477. They were devised in China and subsequently introduced to the west.

The rapid spread of early domestic horses can be traced across Europe, and soon differences in their appearance had arisen. Those kept in northern Europe tended to be small and powerful, not unlike the Exmoor ponies of today, while those in the Middle East were more elegant and larger, perhaps similar to today's Arab horses.

This Egyptian tomb painting reveals the way that horses and their relatives were viewed in ancient times, and the tasks they were expected to perform.

Donkeys and mules

One of the difficulties in accurately determining the dates of the domestication of horses is that, at this stage, there were no characteristic changes in their bone anatomy. Had there been, it would have enabled us to distinguish early domesticated individuals from their wild relatives. The African ass was probably domesticated by the Egyptians at

A Suitable Nature

The natural behavioral characteristics of the horse meant that it was much more receptive to domestication than other members of the equid family. In the wild, horses live together in groups with a stallion, who usually follows watchfully at the back of the herd. In domestication, the part of the stallion is assumed by the handler or rider. This goes some way to explaining why stallions must be gelded, if they are to fit easily within the domesticated group; otherwise, they can be very difficult to manage. Early portrayals of stallions show them reined in with their heads kept high to make sure they cannot resort to a threat gesture, which entails bending their heads forward, which in turn would make them more difficult to control.

Horses were important in battle, as shown by this mosaic of a horse with a Roman charioteer.

BELOW: Horses helped to revolutionize human existence in various ways, not least in terms of agriculture.

RIGHT: The strength of horses has meant they can carry and pull loads that are too heavy for people.

about the same time as the horse, and certainly by 4,500 years ago, donkeys were a common sight in Egypt, carrying people and baskets of goods. There is no doubt, too, that later in the Egyptian era, mules were created by the hybridization of donkeys and horses.

In Roman times, mules were being bred on a relatively large scale, helping to carry equipment for the army throughout the Roman Empire. Writers of this era gave detailed advice on how to breed these hybrids successfully, by fostering a young male donkey, known as a jackass, to a lactating mare. The Romans also had a specially designed platform that allowed male donkeys to mate easily with taller mares.

Hinnies are the result of a mating of a female donkey and a stallion. They can be distinguished from mules by the shape of their head, which is finer, and by the fact that there is long hair only at the tip of the tail, not all the way down as is found in horses.

Perhaps surprisingly, in view of their social structure (see p.14), neither the mountain nor plains zebras have been widely domesticated, although some have been trained to pull carriages. Zebras have been used even less commonly for riding purposes.

ponies
– tough and versatile

Ponies are small horses; the name derives from the French word *poulenet*, which translates as small, male horse. Their origins can be traced back to the Celtic ponies that had emerged in northern and western parts of Europe by the Iron Age. These ponies were not like the breeds of today. They varied quite widely in size, some standing less than about 3 feet (1m) high, but were very strong.

Workers and players

Many of today's pony breeds are linked with areas of northern Europe, where they have lived for many centuries. They include the Shetland, which has been bred for more

ABOVE: *Ponies are ideally suited to younger riders, introducing them to both the skills of riding and the excitement of competitive events.*

LEFT: *A young Exmoor foal. Like other ponies, the Exmoor is relatively hardy, growing a dense, weather-resistant coat at the onset of winter.*

than 2,000 years on the bleak islands of this name located off the coast of Scotland. Ancestral links between the pony breeds and the earliest domesticated horses can be seen in the case of the Highland with its characteristic striped legs and dorsal stripe. This pony is the largest of the British pony breeds, standing approximately 14 hands high (hh).

The Exmoor pony, from the southwest of England, is another ancient breed that has adapted over the course of more than 4,000 years of living on the hard terrain after which it is named. For example, it has a distinctive fan of long hair at the base of its tail, which helps to prevent water from running down and freezing on its hind quarters. Neighboring Dartmoor is also home to a pony breed, once highly valued for carrying tin from the local mines to nearby towns. Many other British pony breeds were used for similar purposes, including the Fells and the Dales, and often displayed remarkable stamina.

Today, many ponies are valued more for their trekking skills than their ability to work, and they have evolved in new environments. The American Shetland, for example, was developed in the nineteenth century from Shetlands crossed initially with Hackney ponies. The Welsh mountain pony laid the foundation for the Australian pony, also in the nineteenth century.

The names of some of the more modern ponies reflect the purpose for which they were bred, rather than revealing anything about their ancestral home. Polo ponies (see p.25) fit into this category, having originated in Argentina, but they have been bred specifically for sport.

What Defines a Pony?

There are physical differences that help to distinguish between horses and ponies. Compared with their body size, ponies have short legs and a more stocky appearance than horses. Their back is often short, with the withers being fairly rounded. They have a broad forehead and a narrow muzzle. The compact shape of ponies means that they are surefooted and surprisingly strong for their size. In addition, they also prove to be very hardy, thanks to their thick winter coat and profuse mane, which give them good protection from the elements.

Like horses, ponies are measured in terms of their height at the withers, which is the highest point of the shoulders. The traditional unit used to measure height is the hand, which is equivalent to 4in (10cm). Ponies must be under 14.2hh (hands high). However, not all equids under this height limit are called ponies; a few, such as the Falabella, are regarded as miniature horses. The Connemara pony (shown below) is particularly hardy, due to its origins in the wild and rough landscape of Galway in western Ireland.

A relatively small head, with an arched neck are characteristics of the Connemara.

Sloping shoulders, creating a good stride length, reveal that Connemara ponies make good mounts.

The Connemara's long tail is set fairly high on the back.

light horses
– supreme riding machines

The anatomy of the horse can have a distinct impact on the comfort, or otherwise, of riding it. Light horses have a back that carries a saddle easily, thanks to the relatively broad, flat structure of their ribs. Their sloping shoulders produce a strong gait, with a long, low movement of the legs. This allows them to cover a lot of ground, with the minimum of effort, with each stride. Coupled with this is a deep chest, which provides for a good lung capacity, enabling these horses to breathe well.

Breeding matters

The origins of many light horses reside in warfare, with some breeds having been developed as cavalry mounts. In addition, a number of horses intended for pulling carriages, such as the Hanoverian (shown opposite), have become widely used for riding. There is also a group of breeds that are valued for their speed, with the oldest lineage tracing back to the Arab and related breeds, such as the Barb. The Arab is believed to have descended from the wild horses that roamed the western part of Asia, although the Caspian is thought to be more closely allied to these original equines. Both the Arab and the Caspian are distinguished by their relatively small head, fine-boned build, and high-set tail.

The Akhal-Teke

The other horse type that made a major contribution to light horse bloodlines originated from central Asia. The environment that these horses had to survive in was fairly inhospitable, with hot summers and freezing winters. As a result, they were athletic and lean, qualities that are reflected in breeds such as the Akhal-Teke, which is from Turkmenistan. The Akhal-Teke was bred initially for racing over 3,000 years ago, and has also displayed tremendous stamina, virtually unmatched in the equine world. In 1935 members of this breed underwent an arduous journey from Ashkhabad to Moscow. This is a distance of 2,500 miles (4,000km), and the trip included a three-day crossing of a desert, without water.

The way in which the Akhal-Teke has adapted to its landscape can be seen in its physical attibutes. Its shoulders are well sloped, producing a very soft gait that assists the breed in walking on sand, while its feet are hard and the associated leg tendons are strong.

The athletic nature of horses is a characteristic that has been refined by selective breeding. Some display more stamina than pace.

A long, fine neck is a characteristic of the Hanoverian, which is a warmblood that is highly valued for show-jumping purposes.

A long, straight back assists the jumping ability of these horses.

This horse is a Hanovarian and shows the typical characteristics associated with the breed.

A deep, broad chest.

The girth is deep, which conveys strength.

Strong, well-balanced limbs contribute to the height of these horses, which can stand up to 16.2 hands high.

Solid joints and well-formed feet. Foot weakness has been eliminated by careful breeding.

U.S.A. and the Morgan

Further development of the domesticated horse has occurred more recently in the Americas. The colonization of North America by Europeans owes much to the horse. If horses had not been available, it is highly unlikely that widespread settlement could have taken place before the advent of mechanized transportation. One of the most important breeds to have evolved in the U.S.A. is the Morgan, which has played a part in the development of many other well-known modern American breeds, including the Saddlebred and Standardbred.

FIGURE AND JUSTIN MORGAN

The origins of the Morgan can be traced back to a single stallion, originally called Figure. His name was changed when he passed into the care of a man called Justin Morgan. Although standing only 14 hands high, the young stallion displayed remarkable strength and stamina, winning weight-pulling contests regularly and never being defeated in a race throughout his entire life. His fame was reflected in the number of mares that he covered during his lifetime, and the Morgan of today reveals the impact that a single outstanding individual can have in terms of influencing the evolution of a breed.

heavy horses
– the ultimate workhorse

Heavy horses, the giants of the horse world, may look intimidating, but in fact they are usually very docile, responsive, and keen to work. Their strength was vital before the age of machines, and even today, in some forested areas, heavy horses are still preferred to vehicles when it comes to dragging out lumber, simply because they can accomplish the task more easily and with less environmental damage.

The largest of heavy horses is the Shire. It can be over 21hh at the withers, and weigh nearly 3,360lb (1,524kg).

Built for strength

As with all horses, good conformation is very important if heavy horses are to be able to work well. Their strength stems from their very powerful, thick neck and broad chest, with their backs being both wide and short. In direct contrast to the light breeds, their stride length is short, with their knees being lifted high, helping them maintain their balance when pulling a load. Pace is of far less

significance. Heavy horses are often described as draught horses, because of their abilities in haulage, whether pulling a plow or a cart.

The origins of this group of horses are unclear, but some members have a very long history, extending back thousands of years, being valued in the Middle Ages as warhorses for carrying knights into battle. The Comtois, for example, with its distinctive light flaxen mane and tail offset against its contrasting dark chestnut coat, was being bred in the region of France after which it was named as early as A.D. 300. Centuries later, the French Emperor Napoleon took them on his ill-fated campaign in Russia. Today, they are still kept for working the land.

There are heavy horse breeds associated with virtually every European country, although it was in China that horses were first kept and worked as teams for plowing, as the result of the development of a special padded collar for this purpose more than 1,500 years ago.

Shire horses plowing a field. The upright shoulders of such horses allow them to be fitted with the necessary collar.

Draft horses are still used for a variety of tasks today, here providing an eye-catching means of delivering beer.

Breed development

There has been much crossbreeding between heavy and light horses down the years. For example, another French heavy horse, the Percheron, was developed through crossings with Arab stallions in a program that began around A.D. 700. This has led to the Percheron having the distinctive concave profile so typical of the Arab. It has also imbued the breed with great stamina, enabling it to cover distances of up to 35 miles (56km) at the trot in a day. In contrast to most heavy horses, it also generally lacks the characteristic longer hair or "feathering" above the hooves, which can become heavily soiled by mud.

The breed that has the most unusual action among all the heavy horses is, however, the Clydesdale (shown below), which originated in the Clyde Valley of Scotland during the mid-1750s. It evolved from local horses and imported heavy horses, including Flemish stock. Subsequently, Shires, too, made a contribution to the breed's development. Clydesdales still have proportionately longer necks than many similar heavy breeds but are particularly distinctive in their high-stepping gait, which looks quite exaggerated compared with other heavy horses. There is no doubting their strength and pulling power, however, a contributing factor being that their withers are higher than their croup.

Some Heavy Breeds	
Ardennais	France
Boulonnais	France
Brabant	Belgium
Breton	France
Clydesdale	Britain
Comtois	France
Døle Gudbrandsdal	Norway
Italian Heavy Draft	Italy
Jutland	Denmark
Muraközi	Hungary
Percheron	France
Russian Heavy Draft	Russia
Shire	Britain
Suffolk Punch	Britain
Vladimir	Russia

Unlike many heavy horses, the Clydesdale has a straight head when viewed in profile.

Longer hair, called feathering, is often present on the feet of heavy horses.

Hock joints lie close together.

The tail is usually decorated with ribbons for shows.

bred for
action

Around the world, particularly in less accessible places, many horses are still kept specifically for work. The breeds used may remain localized, but they are highly valued by those whose livelihoods depend upon them. In remote areas of Tibet, for example, the Tibetan pony has been worked by the local people for centuries. As with so many other breeds, these ponies have evolved to survive very well in their own landscape, having short yet strong legs that enable them to pick their way surefootedly across stony ground or along mountain tracks. They are versatile as well, being used for draft work and as pack animals, in addition to making excellent mounts. So prized were these ponies in the past that they were often presented to Chinese emperors during the Imperial Age.

Hunters

In the west, however, horses have gradually become less necessary for working purposes and are now increasingly used for leisure pursuits. This has led to the creation of horses suitable for particular uses, but not classifiable as a breed.

Although horses will jump instinctively, experience plays a part in giving a safe landing to horse and rider.

Hunters, for example, do not share many common characteristics, because the attributes required for a hunter will vary from region to region, based on the local terrain. For example, open ground calls for speed, with the requirement being for a hunter having a relatively high proportion of Thoroughbred in its ancestry. In areas of more difficult going, however, stamina is likely to be more significant than pace alone. In the show ring, of course, there is a greater tendency toward uniformity, and this has led to distinctions, with show hunters being judged in different classes from working hunters.

The hack and riding pony

The hack is another horse of variable ancestry, although the Thoroughbred tends to predominate in its bloodlines, often along with horses of Anglo-Arab stock. Hacks were originally kept simply for riding, with their looks being significant as well. The scaled-down version of the hack is the "riding pony" of today, in which a strong Arab influence is usually discernible.

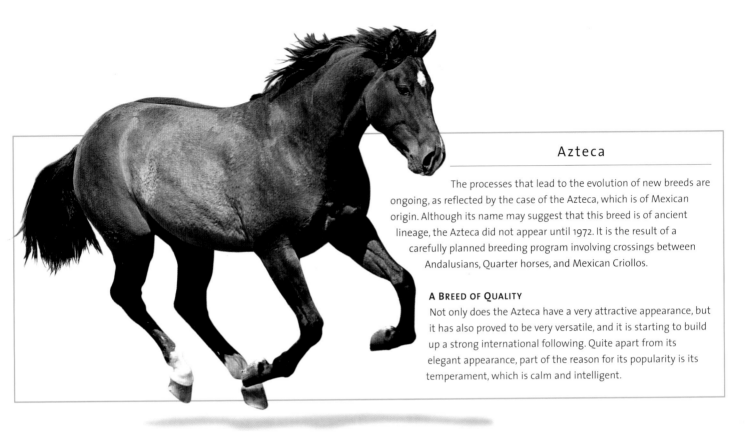

Azteca

The processes that lead to the evolution of new breeds are ongoing, as reflected by the case of the Azteca, which is of Mexican origin. Although its name may suggest that this breed is of ancient lineage, the Azteca did not appear until 1972. It is the result of a carefully planned breeding program involving crossings between Andalusians, Quarter horses, and Mexican Criollos.

A BREED OF QUALITY
Not only does the Azteca have a very attractive appearance, but it has also proved to be very versatile, and it is starting to build up a strong international following. Quite apart from its elegant appearance, part of the reason for its popularity is its temperament, which is calm and intelligent.

Cobs

When it comes to strength and power, the cob is still a popular choice both for hunting and general riding. Such horses usually have some Irish Draught horse in their ancestry, although the Welsh cob may feature in the breeding program as well. A sturdy, deep-chested appearance and relatively short legs are characteristics of the cob, and serve to distinguish these horses, which are also bred to be goodnatured and responsive.

Polo ponies

Selective crossbreeding for sporting purposes has also taken place in the case of the polo pony. These are bred specifically to play polo, an ancient game dating back to about 525 B.C. in Persia. Agility is very important for polo ponies, which need to be able to turn in tight circles. Thoroughbred and Quarter horse crosses often underlie the ancestry of modern polo ponies, which are significantly taller than their ancestors, averaging about 15.1hh.

Polo is popular worldwide, and some of today's best polo ponies come from Argentina.

bred for
color

The basic color of horses is described as dun—a pale yellow-brown with dark mane and tail. The classic dun is Przewalski's horse, which has a yellowish- to reddish-brown coat, offset against its darker mane and tail. This coloration helps disguise wild horses in their natural environment, but nowadays horses occur in a very wide variety of colors and patterns, some of which are associated with a particular breed. The Friesian, a member of the heavy horse group, is always jet black, whereas Quarter horses can be any solid color. There is often confusion over the Palomino because this is both a color recognized in many breeds, and a breed in its own right, members being distinguished by their golden coloration, with contrasting white manes and tails. The Palomino breed was developed in the U.S.A. from Spanish stock.

A Palomino, showing its distinctive coloration, which is characteristic of these horses, as well as being a colour that is seen in other breeds.

The Pinto or Paint

Horses with patterned coats, usually white combined with darker markings, are highly valued for their distinctive camouflage, particularly in the U.S.A., where there are a number of such breeds. The Pinto is well known and has

Appaloosa Coat Colors

Leopard—white over all or part of the body with dark spots on the white
Snowflake—white spotting all over the body
Blanket—white or white-spotted over the hips
Marble—mottled white and dark patterning all over the body
Frost—white specks on a dark coat

OTHER CHARACTERISTICS
● Wispy tail and mane
● White surrounding the iris of the eye
● Mottled skin where it is visible—for example, on the muzzle, eyes, and genitals
● Hooves often vertically striped with black and white

This Appaloosa has a very impressive white blanket patterning over its hindquarters.

Spotted patterning is very closely linked with the Appaloosa.

Blotched patterning is always highly individual, with no two horses displaying identical markings of this type. In some cases, white rather than dark areas predominate.

two basic color forms: the "ovaro," which usually has white areas in the center of its body and elsewhere, offset against large blotches of color, and the "tobiano," which has white, rather than colored, patches predominating in the coat. While all such horses are considered Pintos, there are restrictions based on ancestry, which mean that Paints form a subgroup within the broader Pinto category.

Appaloosas and the Nez Percé Indians

The origins of part-colored horses are believed to lie in Europe, where horses with black-and-white coats are described as piebalds. Other color combinations with white are referred to as skewbalds.

Patterned horses played a significant part in native culture in North America. There the Nez Percé tribe, based in Oregon, were responsible for the development of the Appaloosa. This particular breed of horse is characterized by having more discrete spotted markings than the Pinto.

feral
horses

The word "feral" is used to describe domestic animals that have reverted to living in the wild. Feral horses have a relatively coarse appearance with a large head and usually display considerable stamina. They generally do not settle well into a domesticated lifestyle, however, proving to be difficult to break for riding.

Perhaps the best known feral horses are the Mustangs of North America. Horses were reintroduced to the Americas in 1519. Gradually, as expeditions took place from Europe and settlers arrived, some of these horses escaped and began to spread across the vast North American continent. It was in the southern United States that feral horses first became established. The Native American population of this region, particularly the Comanches and Apaches, did not

A Mustang roundup. Weaned foals have traditionally been caught with lassos and broken for riding.

try to domesticate these feral horses. Instead, they attacked European settlements to steal their stock, which added in due course to the number of feral horses, since not all of these horses were recaptured.

Increase and decline

Numbers of feral horses probably peaked in the late 1700s, when there may have been as many as five million, covering much of the U.S.A. and often in vast herds comprising several thousand individuals. Subsequently, increasing human settlement led to a decline in their numbers, particularly close to developing towns, although it was still not unusual for unwanted domesticated stock to be turned loose, to augment the wild herds, which were left largely unhindered.

The situation changed dramatically as the result of the Boer War in 1899, however, when there was a huge demand for horses to be shipped to southern Africa.

A herd of Mustangs. Their name is derived from the Spanish word "mestena," which means group, although their numbers today are much smaller than in the past.

Australian Brumbies

In Australia the pattern of equine colonization was similar to that which occurred in North America. Horses were introduced to the Australian continent in the late 1800s, and one of the earliest recorded breeders was a Private James Brumby of the New South Wales Corps. When he was transferred to Tasmania, Brumby left his horses behind, and they became feral. As a result, feral horses in Australia today are known as Brumbies, with their population reckoned to be between 125,000 and 205,000. Their numbers may plummet during periods of drought, however, and they are also hunted.

A NATURAL LIFESTYLE
Brumbies normally live in small groups, consisting of a stallion and up to 12 mares, with young colts being driven out when they are aged between a year and 18 months old. Herds display strong territorial instincts; even during times of drought and scarcity of grazing, they are reluctant to move from their home area, which may be up to 60 sq miles (150 sq km). Brumbies still range quite widely through much of Australia, although they are not found in desert areas, nor close to major centers of human settlement.

The African continent is not a good environment for domestic horses because of their susceptibility to disease spread by the tsetse fly and other biting insects. This resulted in high mortality, so the demand for horses continued throughout the war, leading to a dramatic reduction in the feral horse population in the U.S.A.

American military commanders soon realized that they had an asset in these feral horses, which became known as Mustangs, and they released a number of stallions in certain areas, with a view to improving the bloodstock. Large numbers of Mustangs were again rounded up for military service during World War I, but this was to be the last time they were used to any significant extent in combat, as horses were gradually replaced by mechanized transportation. Hunting pressures on herds in the U.S.A. increased during the latter years of the twentieth century, to the extent that estimated numbers have now fallen down to as few as 16,000 individuals.

adapted for
survival

As herbivores, equids are potential prey for a number of carnivorous mammals. Living in herds helps to provide them with some protection, however, since it makes it harder for a predator to creep up on the group without being detected. In some cases, these herds associate with other animals to increase their chances of survival. For example, on the plains of Africa, zebras are often found with giraffes. The long necks and alert nature of the giraffes make them well placed to spot danger from a distance away and raise the alarm. This is of great benefit, since wild horses depend largely on an early warning to outrun a hunter. For example, the cheetah is ideally built for sprinting and can outpace a fleeing zebra over a short distance. However, if the zebra has a sufficient head start, the cheetah will tire and lose interest in the pursuit. Lions pose much more of a threat in this instance, because they will hunt in prides rather than alone. The pursuing lion is likely to attempt to drive its prey toward other pride members lying in ambush.

Instinctively cautious

Equids are cautious at all times, not just when grazing, but also when drinking, and with good reason, particularly in Africa. Here, they may face attacks not just from on the land, but also in the water, because crocodiles may lurk just under the surface, lungeing at the unwary and pulling them to their death. For this reason, zebras and other herd animals have developed a particular strategy at watering places. When a herd approaches the water, not all the individuals will drink simultaneously. They take it in turns, with some remaining watchful for possible danger, just as when they are grazing.

Physical defenses

Once caught by a predator, a horse has few defenses. If cornered, the zebra may lash out with its powerful hindlimbs, which can easily smash a lion's jaw if they make effective contact, but often it will succumb to the attack. Stallions represent a more significant challenge than other members of the herd, and so potential predators, especially lions, will more usually target a young or obviously weakened individual, because it is more likely to be able to outrun it and pull it down more easily than any other.

Disputes between horses can be quite violent affairs, as shown by these zebras. A kick can result in a broken jaw, leading to a slow death from starvation.

The Horse's Senses

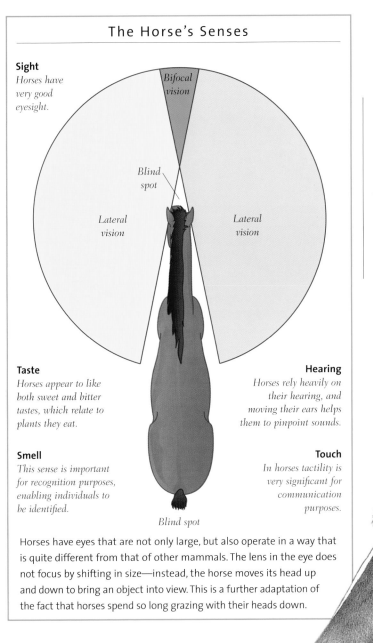

Sight
Horses have very good eyesight.

Bifocal vision

Blind spot

Lateral vision

Lateral vision

Taste
Horses appear to like both sweet and bitter tastes, which relate to plants they eat.

Hearing
Horses rely heavily on their hearing, and moving their ears helps them to pinpoint sounds.

Smell
This sense is important for recognition purposes, enabling individuals to be identified.

Touch
In horses tactility is very significant for communication purposes.

Blind spot

Horses have eyes that are not only large, but also operate in a way that is quite different from that of other mammals. The lens in the eye does not focus by shifting in size—instead, the horse moves its head up and down to bring an object into view. This is a further adaptation of the fact that horses spend so long grazing with their heads down.

covers a large area behind them and the other is directly in front. It is not a good idea to approach a horse from behind, because it may not see you and could be spooked.

Acute hearing

Horses have keen hearing. When listening, their ears point forward, which helps them to locate the sound source accurately. Ear position is also a means of visual communication. By putting its ears back, a horse can indicate that it is fearful, particularly if this is combined with vocal communication such as a snort. Horses rely more on visual than vocal communication.

Brilliant sight

Horses have very acute vision, partly due to the position of their eyes on the sides of the head, which enables them to see almost through 360 degrees. The eyes are also set quite high, so horses are able to drink or graze while still being able to see danger. They have two blind spots—one

Living in open country, horses have evolved particularly acute vision, to warn of danger.

the mechanics
of the horse

The horse is equipped for speed, thanks to its relatively long, powerful legs. It also has a long neck, which allows it to graze easily. The length of the neck comes not from an increase in the number of cervical vertebrae that make up this part of the vertebral column, but rather from an increase in their breadth.

The Thoroughbred is the fastest breed of horse, in terms of its pace. This is primarily due to its long hindlegs and excellent lung capacity.

In total, there are seven cervical vertebrae. The first articulates with the skull and is known as the atlas; the second has a vertical raised area on its upper part for the attachment of muscles and is known as the axis. At the base of the neck, the cervical vertebrae connect with the thoracic vertebrae, which mark the start of the ribcage and the chest. The lumbar vertebrae extend above the abdominal area, providing support for the hip joints, along with the sacrum behind. The tail is made up of coccygeal vertebrae, which taper along their length and mark the end of the vertebral column.

The structure of the horse's vertebral column is very significant as it allows the propulsion provided by the hindlimbs to be transmitted to the forequarters. In addition, it needs to be relatively stable and rigid in order to carry the great bulk of the horse's digestive tract since there is relatively little bony support for it under the body.

The hindlimbs

The horse's speed comes from its well-muscled hindlimbs, although there are very obvious differences in conformation, based on the evolution of the breed or the purposes for which it was created. Tall, slender horses, for example, will have less stamina than those with a broad chest and short, powerful limbs.

Where bones meet, they form joints. The structure of the joints is reinforced by the tough, fibrous ligaments, which extend across the joint, attaching to both bones.

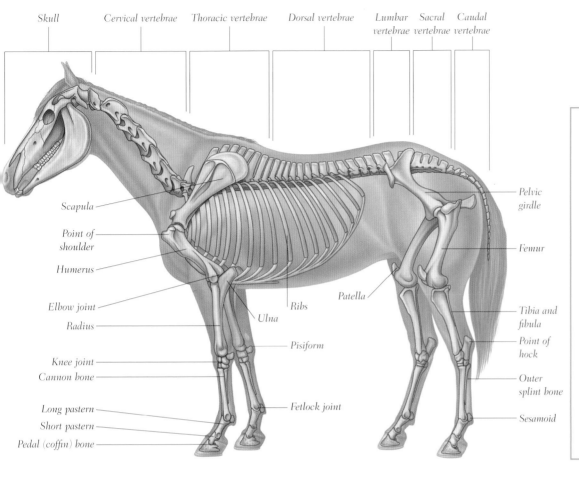

Skull · Cervical vertebrae · Thoracic vertebrae · Dorsal vertebrae · Lumbar vertebrae · Sacral vertebrae · Caudal vertebrae

Scapula
Point of shoulder
Humerus
Elbow joint
Radius
Knee joint
Cannon bone
Long pastern
Short pastern
Pedal (coffin) bone
Ribs
Ulna
Pisiform
Fetlock joint

Pelvic girdle
Femur
Patella
Tibia and fibula
Point of hock
Outer splint bone
Sesamoid

Fact File

• There are 250 bones in a horse's body, although there can be slight differences between breeds.
• The horse's skull alone is comprised of 34 bones in total.
• Typically, 40 teeth are present in the jaws of an adult horse.
• The tallest horse was a Shire, which grew to a height of 21.2hh.
• A Palomino horse called Chinook had the largest tail ever recorded, measuring 22ft (6.7m) in length.
• The mane can grow as long as 18ft (5.5m).

Points of a Horse

The points are the external features of the horse, which contribute to its conformation as well as its appearance, although not its coloration. They are basically a series of terms used to describe different external parts of the body. Although the names of the points are standardized, their relative size and angulation can vary significantly between different breeds. This in turn means that there are significant differences in conformation between, for example, light and heavy horses. These differences can be related to the primary purpose for which the breed was developed.

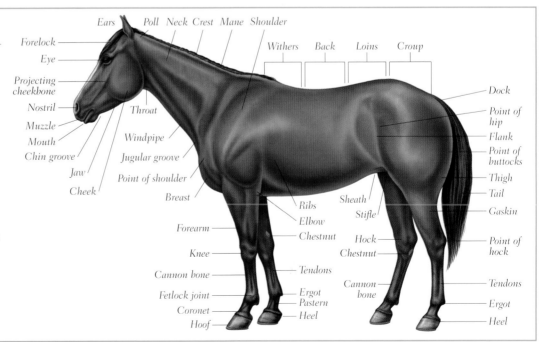

Ears · Poll · Neck · Crest · Mane · Shoulder
Forelock
Eye
Projecting cheekbone
Nostril
Muzzle
Mouth
Chin groove
Jaw
Cheek
Throat
Windpipe
Jugular groove
Point of shoulder
Breast
Forearm
Knee
Cannon bone
Fetlock joint
Coronet
Hoof

Withers · Back · Loins · Croup
Dock
Point of hip
Flank
Point of buttocks
Thigh
Tail
Gaskin
Point of hock
Tendons
Ergot
Heel

Ribs
Elbow
Chestnut
Tendons
Ergot
Pastern
Heel
Sheath
Stifle
Hock
Chestnut
Cannon bone

The elasticity within the ligaments ultimately determines the degree of flexibility at the joint itself. Tendons also attach to the bones, helping to bind the muscles and preventing them from tearing apart.

The pelvic girdle provides the support at the rear of the horse's body, with the head of the femur fitting into the cup to produce the hip joint. The lower end of the femur forms the stifle, the point at which the hind limb becomes clearly defined. In front of the stifle, there is a separate smaller bone, known as the patella, which corresponds to the human kneecap and aids the stifle's movement.

Below the stifle is the tibia and its smaller, thinner companion, the fibula. Together these extend down to the hock joint. This middle part of the leg provides stability, because the muscle groups located here are shared by the hock and the stifle. The horse cannot flex its stifle without flexing the hock at the same time.

The hock joint is complex, consisting of the small tarsal bones bound tightly together by ligaments. Externally, however, it should feel relatively smooth on each side of the leg. Any swelling here could be a sign of abnormalities affecting the joint, such as spavins or curbs, which in turn will detract from the soundness of the horse. Below the hock, the cannon bone extends down to the pastern where there is a joint, corresponding to our ankle and called the fetlock. The pastern bones should show a moderate slope, and this part of the leg must be of medium length, if it is to act effectively as the shock-absorber for the foot.

The forelegs
The forelegs do not have a bony attachment to the body; instead, ligaments and muscle bind the upper part of the leg, which includes the flattened scapula, to the sides of the chest. This, too, helps to absorb the stresses of

LEFT: *A huge international bloodstock industry has grown up in centers such as Newmarket in England.*

RIGHT: *Heavy horses are built for power rather than speed, as displayed by this Shire. Their bodies are heavily muscled, and their legs thick and strong.*

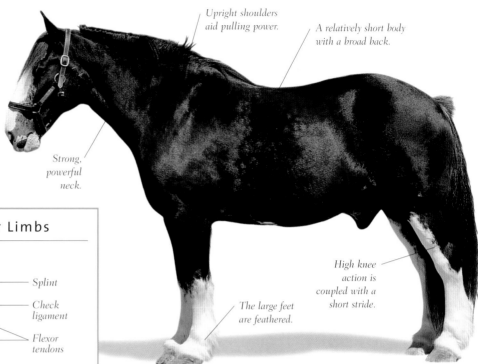

Upright shoulders aid pulling power.

A relatively short body with a broad back.

Strong, powerful neck.

High knee action is coupled with a short stride.

The large feet are feathered.

The Structure of the Lower Limbs

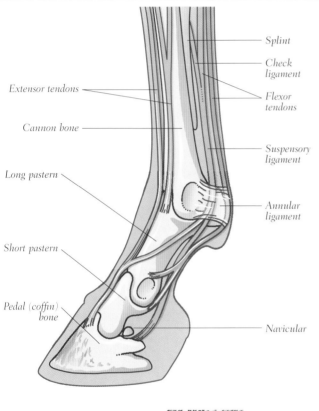

Extensor tendons

Cannon bone

Long pastern

Short pastern

Pedal (coffin) bone

Splint

Check ligament

Flexor tendons

Suspensory ligament

Annular ligament

Navicular

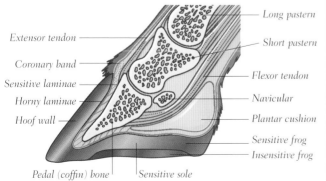

Extensor tendon

Coronary band

Sensitive laminae

Horny laminae

Hoof wall

Pedal (coffin) bone

Long pastern

Short pastern

Flexor tendon

Navicular

Plantar cushion

Sensitive frog

Insensitive frog

Sensitive sole

movement at speed. Otherwise, the structure of the foreleg is similar to that of the hindleg, with the knee replacing the hock. Roughened areas on the inside of the leg just above the knees are normal: called chestnuts, they are the remains of a digit lost during evolution. Chestnuts are also found on the hindlegs just below the hock.

The foot

The shape of the horse's foot comes from the pedal bone. Shape varies somewhat according to the type of horse, with the heavy breeds having not just larger, but also flatter, feet than the lighter breeds. With all breeds, however, it is important that there are no cracks or ridges evident in the hoof. When the foot is lifted up to show the sole, it should be possible to see the distinction between the outer horn wall, into which the shoes are fixed, and the sensitive inner part. Shoeing, which is carried out on most domesticated horses, prevents the hooves from being worn down from work on hard surfaces, such as asphalt. Shoes need to be changed every month to six weeks, and must be made specifically to fit the individual horse's feet.

different gaits
different speeds

The word "gait" is used to describe the way in which the horse is moving, and its pace. Horses generally display four distinct gaits of increasing pace. The first investigation into the way they move was carried out in Victorian times by the photographer Eadweard Muybridge, who took a series of exposures of horses at different speeds, and so revealed key differences in the sequence in which the legs move during the various gaits.

Pacing

Other gaits have also been created in association with certain breeds. Pacing is typically associated with horses being kept for harness racing and is a two-beat gait, with the legs moving in corresponding pairs, starting on the left side of the body and followed by the right side. Harness racing is especially popular in the U.S.A. where it draws large numbers of spectators. The race track is usually 1 mile (1.6km) long, and the horses often complete the course in under two minutes.

Harness racing is very popular in the U.S.A. The American Standardbred has been evolved for this sport, which can draw huge crowds.

THE WALK

The slowest of the four gaits is the walk. In the walk, two or sometimes three feet are on the ground simultaneously. The steps are even, so the footfall sounds even. The sequence begins with the left (or "near") hind, followed by the matching forefoot, then the right (or "off") hind and the corresponding forefoot. The sequence then continues with the left fore, right hind, right fore, and left hind. The Tennessee Walking horse has a very different walking gait. Two distinct walking paces—the flat walk and the running walk—are recognized in this case, both of which are four-beat paces, with the hind feet extending in front of the corresponding front hoof prints.

THE TROT

When the horse starts to move at a faster pace than walking, this is described as trotting. The legs in this case move in diagonal pairs, beginning with the left fore and right hind, which creates the first beat, followed by the right fore and left hind, creating the second. The rider is thrown up a short distance from the saddle in this gait, and then lands back down gently. There are a number of trotting horses with a specialized gait, including French and Russian Trotters. A long stride length is very important in these horses, allowing them to cover the ground well. Strong, powerful legs also tend to be characteristic of such horses, which are used for racing purposes.

THE CANTER

Faster still is the canter, a three-beat gait, during which, for a brief period of time all the feet are off the ground (suspension). Cantering on the right lead starts with the right foreleg, followed by the left hind, and then the so-called left diagonal movement, involving both the right hind and left fore, and finally the right fore, after which the period of suspension occurs before the sequence is repeated. Horses can also canter on the left lead. In this case, the gait begins with the left fore, followed by the right hind, then the left hind and right fore, with, finally, the left fore. Cantering is the last pace at which it is possible to make out the sequence of the individual hooves falling.

THE GALLOP

Galloping is the horse's fastest pace, during which often only one foot hits the ground at a time, and never more than two. Thoroughbreds are the fastest horses in the world and can reach speeds equivalent to 43mph (70kph). The posture of the rider is altered at gallop. By leaning forward in the saddle, rather than sitting upright, the rider allows the horse to move more freely, with the weight being more evenly distributed along the horse's back. Two distinct sequences can occur during galloping. One starts with the left fore, then right fore, followed by the left hind and right hind; the other starts with the right fore, left fore, right hind, and left hind.

A horse will normally walk readily, but you need to be alert, because if it is spooked, it is likely to speed up very quickly.

Trotting is known as a two-beat gait, because of the way in which the legs work in diagonal pairs.

Good balance is an important feature of cantering, and this applies to the rider as well as the horse.

Note the marked extension in the positioning of the forelimbs, which is a feature of galloping.

teeth
and teething problems

The herbivorous diet of the horse has had a major impact on its appearance, particularly its head, since the jaws need to be large and powerful to accommodate the deep-rooted teeth and associated musculature necessary for chewing grass. The incisor teeth are located at the front of the mouth and used for plucking herbage. Behind them may be canine teeth, known as tushes, although these do not always develop in mares, and there is then a gap known as the diastema. The diastema allows the horse to pluck new vegetation and keep it separate from food already in its mouth that it wants to chew. Farther up, toward the back of the jaw, are the premolars, followed by the molars or cheek teeth.

Horses have two sets of teeth through their lives: foals are born with milk (or deciduous) teeth, which are gradually replaced by permanent dentition up to the age of about five years. Adult horses typically have 40 teeth, consisting of 12 incisors, four canines, 12 premolars, and 12 molars, although the number and size of the canines (tushes) is variable. Similarly, the first premolar or wolf tooth may only be evident in the upper jaw.

Aging by teeth

The teeth continue to grow throughout a horse's life. A number of alterations occur in the incisors as the horse becomes older, and these provide a means for aging an individual. The changes relate to the structure of the crowns, with the different layers in the tooth wearing down at different rates, as well as to the sides of the teeth, which show different characteristics above the gum line as the tooth grows. In young horses, the remains of the "cup",

The teeth help to provide valuable insight into a horse's approximate age.

Teeth Development

As the foal starts to switch to a solid diet, it becomes increasingly dependent on its teeth. It sheds the milk teeth, which are replaced by its permanent teeth that will last throughout the rest of the horse's life. Grass is plucked by the incisor teeth protruding from the front of the mouth, and is then ground up by the premolars and molars, which can suffer heavy wear as a result. This is why the teeth gradually wear down with age.

CONSEQUENCES OF DENTAL WEAR
The degree of wear on the teeth indicates a horse's age by the changes apparent here. Ultimately, however, if the horse's teeth wear right down, it can have difficulty in eating, which affects its life expectancy, particularly in the case of wild horses.

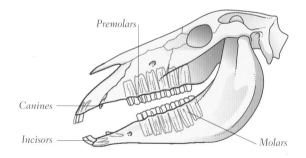

Mature Horse
The jaw of a mature horse has 12 premolars and 12 molars (for grinding) as well as 12 incisors (for biting). By this stage, the roots of the premolar and molar teeth in the jaws greatly exceed the crown above the gum line.

Crib biting is a vice that causes horses to bite on hard surfaces, such as the stable door. It can lead on to wind-sucking (see p.158).

caused by dental cement, is apparent as a streak on the surface of the incisors, but as the tooth becomes worn down, so a second, more circular, mark becomes apparent behind it. Formed by exposure of the pulp cavity, this is known as the dental star. By the time a horse is about 12 years old, the final vestiges of the cup will have eroded, leaving just the dental star visible. In horses of about nine years old, a groove appears on the outside of the third incisor, being apparent at the margin with the gum at this stage. This is called Galvayne's groove, and it provides a further means of aging a horse. As the tooth grows because of wear on its surface, the groove gradually extends. When the horse is 15 years old, Galvayne's groove has reached halfway down the tooth, taking five more years to reach the cutting edge. After this, it starts to wear away, disappearing from the base of the tooth.

The Horse Dentist

Dental care in the domesticated horse is very important as sharp edges occur on the upper molars and lower premolars because the teeth do not align exactly. This is due to the horse's jaw structure, with the lower jaw being narrower than the upper. The sharp edges have to be removed by rasping every six months or so.

Apart from regular visits, it is also time to call the dentist when:
● Your horse drops partially chewed food from his mouth on a regular basis. Known as quidding, this indicates pain in the mouth.
● He dislikes being touched on the cheeks or pulls away when you stroke the sides of his head.
● When being bridled, he shows reluctance to take the bit in his mouth, or reacts badly to having the noseband fastened.
● On being ridden, he appears resistant to the bit.
● He seems to be losing condition despite being well fed or being in good pasture.

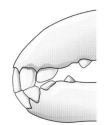 

Flat, oval tables and long, small cups

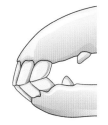 

Round tables and oval cups

 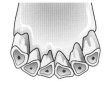

Triangular tables and rounded cups

Five Years
At five years old, the milk teeth have been replaced by permanent incisors and molars, and cup marks appear on the tooth surface, or table.

Twelve Years
At 12 years old, the teeth have begun to slope outward and cup marks are less distinct; the dental star is still visible.

Old Age
In old age, the outward slope of the teeth is very pronounced, and Galvayne's groove has almost entirely disappeared.

the anatomy of
eating

Horses have to spend long periods grazing each day to meet their nutritional needs.

The food a horse eats is generally of low nutritional value, so it has to consume large quantities to meet its needs. As a result, horses spend a great deal of their time eating. In a typical day, they will consume roughly 2 percent of their body weight, in contrast to carnivores in the wild, which may not even eat every day.

To cope with this huge and constant intake of food, a horse requires not only strong teeth, but also a large digestive tract. The digestive process begins in the mouth, where the teeth break down the herbage, and saliva starts chemical digestion. Horses produce large volumes of saliva, typically about 24 pints (11 litres) daily.

The food mix passes into the stomach and through the small intestine, being exposed to further enzymes here. The blind-ending sac, known as the cecum, marks the division between the large and small intestines. It has a key role to play in the digestive process, because it is here that beneficial bacteria and protozoa act to break down the cellulose present in plant matter. Absorption, mainly of vitamins and water, occurs in the large intestine, after which waste matter passes out of the body as feces.

The problem of laminitis

Unfortunately, since they are so dependent on microbes to assist the digestive process, horses have great difficulty in coping with sudden dietary changes, and any such changes may have an adverse effect. For example, ponies allowed on to lush grass are likely to suffer from the foot condition laminitis, caused by inflammation of the laminae in the hoof (see p.35). Severe cases of laminitis can lead to a shift in position of the pedal bone, with the front feet being most vulnerable. It is intensely painful, and affected animals usually try to stand with the weight shifted as far as possible to the back of their hooves. Inflammation

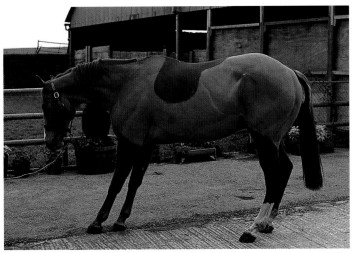

causes the feet to feel hot, and the pony will also be reluctant to move. Painkillers and dietary adjustments are needed, and once an animal has suffered from this condition, recurrences are not uncommon.

Coping with colic

Colic, too, is intensely painful, and affects the abdomen. It is often linked with diet, as well as parasitic worms that are present within the intestinal tract. Affected horses are distressed, rolling more than usual and kicking their abdominal area in an attempt to relieve the problem. Sweating and constipation are other signs, along with an increase in the horse's respiratory rate. Veterinary advice needs to be sought without delay in such cases. In some cases of colic, the gut will be twisted, and surgery is likely to be necessary.

Dear Equine Casebook

I have just had a horse suffer from colic. It was a horrible experience for both of us, and for a while it was touch-and-go whether he would survive. How do I make sure it will never happen again?
Yours truly, Frank Williams

Colic can be a life-threatening condition, but you can greatly reduce the risks by sensible management. Never be tempted to feed your horse just before or immediately after exercise, and always carry out regular deworming, based on your veterinarian's advice. Horses have relatively small stomachs and need to be fed in small amounts throughout the day, with their diets being changed gradually over the course of several days, rather than suddenly. Bulky rations are vital, so if your horse does not have access to grass, it is important that it receives adequate quantities of good-quality hay or haylage. Hay needs to be sweet-smelling and slightly green. Never feed excessively dusty or moldy hay, which is also likely to harm your horse's health.

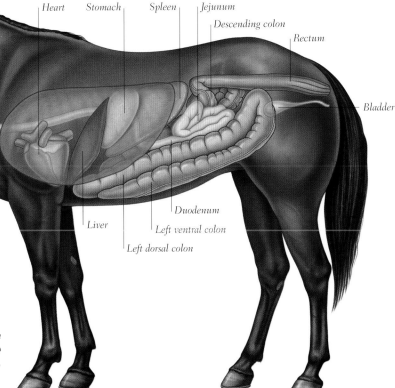

Esophagus
Heart *Stomach* *Spleen* *Jejunum*
Descending colon
Rectum
Bladder
Liver
Duodenum
Left ventral colon
Left dorsal colon

The horse's high fiber intake requires a correspondingly large digestive system to cope with the amount of bulk.

a close-knit **community**

In a number of parts of the world, horses still range freely over areas of open land. In the southwest of England, for example, Exmoor is home to one of the oldest pony breeds in the world, while farther east, in the New Forest, ponies have lived continuously in a state of what could be termed "semi-liberty" since the tenth century.

Mutual grooming

Within these herds, behavior patterns clearly associated with those of their wild ancestors can often be seen. It is quite easy to recognize individuals that are closely related, since they will often engage in mutual grooming. This is when two horses nuzzle up to each other and then one, or both, gently nibbles at the coat of its companion. Grooming like this can last for several minutes at a time. The areas of the body chosen for grooming are not random; they are associated with parts of the autonomic nervous system, and this type of behavior appears to have a calming effect on the horses involved, which results in a measurable lowering of their heart rates.

ABOVE: There are strong bonds that exist within a herd of horses, with herd members able to recognize their companions with at difficulty.

LEFT: The bond between mare and foal is reinforced by mutual grooming, which consequently has a social as well as a practical function.

Grooming behavior may also be seen in horses living in a field, although the bonds between these animals may not be as strong as those between members of a semi-wild herd. Studies have shown that firm bonding can be achieved by removing two horses from a herd and keeping them together, but in isolation from the main group, for a minimum period of two weeks. During this time, they will form a close relationship, which will be retained even if they are then reintroduced to the larger group.

Homing instinct
If a horse is cut off from from the herd, it can usually rejoin them in much the same way that a domesticated horse can find its way home. This ability depends partly on being in a familiar landscape and also on the fresh trail left by others in the herd. When seeking out its herd, a horse will actually follow in their footprints where possible, as well as using its sense of smell to sniff the correct path when there are no obvious visual clues.

A stallion chases off a younger rival seeking to displace him as the herd leader. Conflicts of this type can sometimes lead to serious fighting.

alarm call to others nearby, being made within seconds of the sighting.

Tail swishing

Unlike that of a dog, the horse's tail is not significant for communication purposes. However, it does have a very important function, which is particularly obvious during hot weather: it acts as a fly swish, with the horse flicking it to and fro to deter insects from landing on its body. Aside from causing irritation, some flies will bite through the horse's skin, causing inflammation and infection. Horses will often group together under trees and in other more shaded areas when the sun is at its hottest, standing nose to tail, so that the swish of one horse's tail also helps to deter flies from landing on its neighbor's head.

Scent is very important in horses, helping to maintain the stability within the herd. Stallions living in the wild will defecate in piles, which serve as both visual and olfactory indicators that they are occupying the territory; they also mask the droppings of their mares by urinating and defecating in the same spot, having sniffed the area first.

Vocal communication

It is possible for horses to keep in touch with each other by means of their calls, with some sounds being audible over a much greater distance than others. Vocal communication is not of very great importance to horses, however, since they have evolved to live in grassland, where their large size means they tend to be visible from far off. As far as a herd's wellbeing is concerned, the most significant sound in their repertoire is undoubtedly the "blow": this is made by the horse blowing air through its nose and can be audible over 656ft (200m) away. A blow is uttered almost instinctively when a herd member unexpectedly encounters an unfamiliar object or creature, and serves as a rapid

The language of stallions

The natural behavior of stallions, particularly communication between rivals, is unlikely to be seen in the field environment, simply because they are difficult to manage, and keeping two together is not recommended. In the wild, however, the subtle changes that occur as the breeding season approaches can be observed from a safe distance. For example, an established stallion may be challenged by a younger rival. Initially, a ritual of body language will be used which sends out strong messages that will often resolve the matter, with fighting occurring only as the last resort. In fact, the vast majority of encounters end without

Horses like this Exmoor pony will only lie down when they feel secure, usually with other herd members standing nearby to warn of approaching danger.

overt physical violence being displayed. Even then, the conflict tends to be brief: the stallions will circle each other and may paw at the ground nervously before one rears up, lungeing out with its front feet, which can inflict a serious blow on a rival. Stallions will also use their teeth. When the weaker individual backs down, he will be chased well away from the mares, although the combat has essentially ended by this stage.

Mares and the herd hierarchy

An order of dominance also exists between the mares in a herd, but this may be less obvious for much of the year. Mares with foals tend to be more protective and thus aggressive, and so move up the social hierarchy, at least on a temporary basis. Unfortunately, when a mare becomes particularly aggressive, it can create problems, not least because the foal itself may end up being inadvertently injured as the mare rushes toward a potential threat. Such behavior is most commonly seen soon after birth, with most mares becoming less protective as their offspring grow older. The risk of injury to the young horse under these circumstances is obviously lessened outdoors in a paddock rather than within the confines of a stall.

Lying down and rolling

Other natural behavior in horses includes lying down to doze, and rolling. In spite of their size, horses lie down only when they feel secure in their surroundings. It is much more common for them to sleep standing up, effectively napping for short intervals. This not only allows them to become aware of predators more quickly, but also means they are in the best position to escape if danger threatens. If they are caught lying down, they are disadvantaged by the relatively slow process of standing up, as well as the inability to strike out with their hooves. Horses are well-equipped with what is known as the "stay apparatus" in their legs, which allows them to remain standing for long periods, while minimizing the muscular effort required.

Dear Equine Casebook

Why does my horse keep rolling on her back? When I ride her, I give her a good grooming before turning her out in the field, but she always goes straight for the muddiest patch and rolls until she is filthy.
Yours truly, Emma Firth

On occasion, horses will roll on the ground. This sort of behavior is more likely to be seen when a horse has recently been turned out into a field than among wild or semi-wild herds. Rolling is rather similar to our desire to stretch, and allows your horse to tone up her back muscles after being ridden or standing in a stable for a while. Repeated and agitated rolling is, however, a typical symptom of the intestinal complaint known as colic (see p.41), particularly if the horse attempts to kick its belly with its hooves, and requires veterinary assistance.

courtship
and the reproductive process

Horses mature at a relatively early age, with stallions often attaining sexual maturity at just 18 months, and mares about six months later, although in domestic circumstances they are not normally allowed to breed until they are three or four years old, by which stage they will be fully developed. In the wild, bands of young stallions often do not begin breeding until they are quite a bit older, usually starting to do so when they are strong enough to maintain and defend their own harems.

The breeding season

The breeding period extends from early spring through until late summer, which, in the case of the northern hemisphere, means that mares come into season between February and August; the peak months are April to June. The response is triggered by increasing day length and rising temperatures. Provision of artificial daylight and increased temperature are used to bring Thoroughbred mares into season in January to make sure that foals are born as close to January 1 as possible—gestation being approx-

Flehmening is a very distinctive gesture, usually carried out by stallions, with the lips being extended forward rather than drawn back.

imately 340 days. This is to tie in with the racing calendar, which takes a horse's birthday to be January 1. (A youngster born soon after the beginning of the year will have a distinct advantage when raced against one born later in the season.)

Normally, the breeding cycle serves to make sure that foals will be produced at a time when there is likely to be plenty of good grazing for them, which in turn will allow them to develop well before the onset of winter.

Flehmening

When a mare is coming into season, she emits pheromones (chemical molecules), which are carried through the air and indicate her reproductive state. A stallion can detect this olfactory cue by a behavioral response known as flehmening. He curls back his upper lip, effectively sucking air into his mouth, which passes over something called Jacobson's organ. This is located in the roof of the mouth and connects directly to the olfactory center in the brain. The stallion may also sniff at a mare's urine in a similar way, as well as her vulva. Flehmening is linked to sexual behavior and is distinct from smelling, for which the nostrils are used. On occasion, however, particularly when feeding your horse something that it has not encountered before, such as a herbal treat perhaps, it may also curl up its lips in this fashion. Such behavior may be linked to memory with the horse seeking to identify an unfamiliar scent that it does not immediately recognize.

On stud farms where the stallion is kept separated from the mares, teasing is carried out to see whether a mare is ready to be mated. Otherwise, she could react aggressively, which could injure the stallion.

Where stallions and mares are run in natural herds, there is a period of courtship before mating takes place.

Covering

A mare comes into season and is receptive to a stallion at intervals of approximately three weeks up until the time she falls pregnant. The estrous period itself lasts five days, and there are behavioral signs that indicate when a mare is ready to mate. She often spends more time associating with other horses, but will not hesitate to rebuff the attentions of a stallion if she is not yet ready. As a result, in domestic situations, mating has to be carefully timed, and often, a so-called "teaser" stallion is used to determine whether a mare is ready to permit mating, and only then will the chosen stud be brought forward. In the wild, a receptive mare will mate repeatedly, as frequently as once an hour, over the course of the next two or three days.

pregnancy
and the birth

There is usually a slight variance in the length of the pregnancy, which lasts just over 11 months, depending on the gender of the foal, with the gestation period for colts often being a couple of days longer than for fillies. Twin pregnancies are very uncommon in horses, and if conceived, they rarely go to term, simply because the mare is unable to meet the requirements of two foals in her uterus.

During the early stages of her pregnancy, the mare will not increase noticeably in size, since putting on a significant amount of weight at this stage would be a handicap in the wild. Instead, the development of the foal and its body organs occurs during the first eight months or so. The major growth spurt happens in the final three months, when additional food is very important.

Two months after the mare is covered, the gender of the foal is clearly apparent, and the limbs are formed, although it will be another two months before the hooves are obvious. At this stage, the young horse weighs 2 pounds (1kg). In another four months, its weight will have increased to about

40lb (19kg) and it will measure about 28in (71cm) long. Ten months after mating, the foal will be almost fully developed, with a full coat and mane and tail evident. The birth weight of a typical foal lies between 85 and 107lb (38.5 and 48.5kg), and its length will be at least 43in (109cm).

Pregnancy Chart

Month 2—The body shape of the young foal is already apparent, and it is possible to distinguish its sex at this age.

Month 4—The hooves are well-defined by this stage, and signs of hair are visible, especially around the muzzle.

Month 6—By now the young foal is well covered with hair over its entire body, although the mane is not yet developed.

Month 8—The mane of the foal in the uterus is now beginning to grow, but there is little hair on the tail. The body weight of the foal is increasing.

Month 10—This is the major growth phase of the foal in the uterus, and its weight increases rapidly from now through to the end of pregnancy.

Month 11—With birth imminent, the foal's position shifts so it can be born head first, with its front legs extended.

Pregnancy

It is usually not possible to tell visually until about eight months after covering occurred that the mare is pregnant because, up to this point, the foal is small in size. This is the stage at which the amount of food offered to the mare will need to be increased to take account of the foal's spurt in growth. Even so, it is important to be aware that covering was successful before this, since it is not a good idea to ride a pregnant mare in the latter half of her pregnancy. Using an ultrasound scan, pregnancy can be detected as early as 12 days after mating, but generally this technique is used from three weeks on. Blood testing between 45 and 120 days after mating is an alternative.

Four months

Eight months

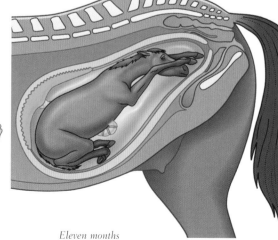
Eleven months

Foals are normally born head first, with the vast majority of mares giving birth lying down rather than standing.

In the wild, it is vital that young horses are up on their feet and able to move as soon as possible after birth.

Birth

Just prior to the start of the birth, the foal's position alters, and the uterine contractions begin. The only external sign that birth is imminent may be a waxy secretion on the mare's mammary glands. The fluid present in the allantoic sac, which enveloped and protected the foal from trauma during pregnancy, will break and pour out of the mare's vulva as the contractions become more intense. The mare becomes increasingly restless, lying down and sweating.

Under normal circumstances, the foal's front feet are the first part of the body to emerge, with the head between them. Once the shoulders have passed through the birth canal, the rest of the body emerges very rapidly. The umbilical attachment, which nourished the foal during pregnancy, is then torn, and this separates the young horse from the placenta. The mare will then start to lick her offspring, helping to make sure that its coat dries. She will also encourage the foal to stand. Within 30 minutes of birth, the foal should begin suckling. The placenta passes out of the mare's body anything up to four hours after the birth. Veterinary assistance must be sought if it does not appear, because it will otherwise cause a serious infection.

development
of the foal

It is vital that the foal starts suckling as soon as possible after birth: any delay could affect its chances of survival. This is because the "first milk" or colostrum produced by mares contains proteins called immunoglobulins that will give the young foal protection against infections until its own immune system is fully functional. If it is deprived of this, the foal is likely to be more sickly and its growth may be stunted. The time factor is important, since a foal can only benefit from colostrum for the first 18 hours of its life; after this it cannot absorb the protective proteins. If a foal is unable to feed, the mare may have to be milked to obtain the thick yellowish colostrum, so it can be given directly to her offspring, either from a bottle or through a stomach tube. Subsequently, the foal will feed from its mother around the clock, and the mare will be drinking more water to compensate for the amount of fluid being

Foal Development

1 Day Old—Foal is standing and suckling without problems.
2 Weeks Old—Already used to the presence of people, the foal is becoming used to a leather foal slip, and being led.
6 Weeks Old—Should be growing well and active. May even start to sample some solid food for the first time.

8 Weeks Old—Foal now eating more concentrates, rather than mother's milk and grazing.
12 Weeks Old—Farrier required to trim the foal's feet for the first time. Becomes used to being loaded into a box with its mother.
26 Weeks Old—Foal will have lost its furry milk hairs and be ready to be weaned from its mother.

used for the production of her milk. Milk output varies depending on the breed, but in the case of Thoroughbreds is typically 1–2 gal (4–8 liters) daily.

When the foal is born, it has feces in its intestines, which should be expelled from its body within 12 hours of the birth. The consumption of colostrum helps to trigger this process since it encourages gut activity, but if the so-called meconium has not been produced by this stage, an enema may be necessary. The meconium differs signifi-

A mare will suckle her foal until it is at least six months old in the case of domestic horses, and for as long as 18 months in the wild.

Foals lying asleep, under the protection of their mothers. Even in domestication mares are happiest rearing their foals in groups, rather than on their own.

possible to wean foals in batches, rather than individually, and subsequently allowing the youngsters to stay together.

Whinnying

The bond between a mare and her foal is reinforced by whinnying. This is a relatively high-pitched call, audible over some distance, and studies have revealed that mares will respond more frequently to the whinnying of their own offspring than of other foals. Whinnying is also recognized within the structure of herds of feral horses, as a means of identifying group members, with stallions responding to such calls made by foals and their mothers.

cantly from normal horse droppings in being black and harder than usual. When the mare comes into season again after giving birth, the consistency of her milk changes during this period, and it can result in the foal suffering from a bout of diarrhea.

Weaning

From about six months on, the volume of the mare's milk declines, and this marks the start of the weaning process. In domesticated animals, weaning is normally carried out between six and eight months of age, before the onset of winter. It is important that any young colts are removed from the group before they are a year old, because although they will not be sexually mature by this age, they are likely to be showing signs of sexual behavior, which can prove disruptive.

Weaning can be a difficult time in a foal's life and needs to be carried out carefully to minimize the risk of any long-term problems. Results are often better if it is

Weaning foals together in groups proves less traumatic than separating one off alone.

opting for ownership

2

Keeping a horse is an expensive and time-consuming undertaking, and you do not need to own one to be able to ride frequently, either at a riding school or on one that you have borrowed. However, once you decide that you wish to have your own horse, it is important to choose one whose character you like; all horses are individuals and have their own distinct personality. A good bond between horse and rider is most apparent in the field of competition, with close collaboration vital for success. Of course, fitness is also important, as is the horse's conformation, which can have a significant impact on your chances in a discipline. Equally, understanding the way in which a horse sees the world is necessary to help you get the best performance from it.

is buying
for you?

While owning a horse might be your dream, buying the right one can be fraught with difficulties, and making a purchase is definitely not something to rush into—mistakes can be both costly and distressing. If you make the wrong choice, you will have the trauma of deciding whether to sell your new horse or to try to deal with the problems that have arisen. For example, if you buy a horse that turns out to have an underlying medical problem, it can be very expensive in terms of veterinary bills. It will also have an impact on the extent to which the animal can be ridden. And, throughout, you will have to meet the costs of keeping the horse, too. It is not just a matter of feeding costs, either: there will be regular shoeing, worming, and vaccinations to budget for, as well as equipment, such as blankets and saddlery.

Having your own horse is a year-round commitment. Bear in mind that, whatever the weather, your horse will require attention every day.

Loans

If you do not want the responsibilities attached to owning a horse or pony, it is possible to opt for a loan arrangement, which in effect means sharing a mount owned by someone else, in return for a contribution to its maintenance costs. Although this arrangement may seem appealing, it is not without potential friction. For example, problems can arise when one rider wants to go to a show on the same day as the other rider is planning to enter an event elsewhere. Of course, these difficulties can be avoided by having a comprehensive written agreement, which is strongly advisable in any case. Perhaps the most satisfactory type of loan is when a horse is being kept solely for hacking.

Benefits of Buying
- The horse becomes your property.
- You can ride your horse whenever you want.
- You can enter events of your own choice.
- You can breed from your horse if you wish to.

Benefits of Loaning
- You will not have to pay out to buy the horse.
- You can see how you fare, with no long-term commitment.
- You may be able to split the costs of caring for the horse.
- You may be able to have a better horse than you could afford to buy.

Where to keep your horse

If, despite the drawbacks, you decide to acquire a horse, the first consideration must be where you will keep it. While you may be in the fortunate position of having your own land, there may still be significant costs involved in making it suitable for a horse. You will need to consider the construction of suitable stabling and safe fencing, not overlooking the cost of supplying water. If you do not have land, you will need to make other arrangements for the care of your horse. For many people, this means finding a suitable livery stable.

If you opt for full livery, the staff at the yard will care for your horse, but this will be expensive compared with a part-livery arrangement.

If you are lucky enough to have learned to ride in the area and have a riding school that you have been visiting on a regular basis, you will already have met a number of people locally who are involved with horses, and you can ask them to recommend a nearby livery yard. It could be that your local riding stable does liveries, which might be ideal. A word of warning—although it may be an appealing way of reducing the cost, think carefully before agreeing to letting your horse be used for general hacking by those attending the riding school. This could affect its performance with you; it may start to develop unwanted vices or even go lame. Another possibility, when it comes to finding suitable accommodation, is simply to look in the telephone book, and call some of the yards listed. Arrange to visit the premises to see the facilities on offer before reaching a final decision. Clean surroundings, well-maintained buildings, and enthusiastic staff are obviously all good indicators that the yard is suitable.

In terms of costs, there are usually two options available—part and full livery. In the case of a part livery, you have to undertake some of the work yourself, which should be clearly agreed in advance. This is cheaper than a full livery, where the staff will look after all your horse's needs for you. Should you work unpredictable hours or travel regularly, opting for full livery removes many of the practical worries associated with buying your own horse.

Equipment You Will Need

There is a huge range of equipment available, which can add considerably to the expense of having a horse. Be selective about what you buy, but do not scrimp on safety. You may be able to buy some items second-hand, but check their condition carefully. Always purchase new helmets.

- A head collar.
- A suitable saddle that fits your horse properly; safety stirrups are recommended.
- A numnah pad to fit under the saddle.
- A girth to hold the saddle securely on the horse's body.
- A bridle with a bit and reins.
- Boots and traveling bandages.
- Grooming equipment.
- Blankets, sheets for all-year use.
- A pair of riding boots.
- A riding helmet conforming to the latest safety standards.
- A whip and possibly gloves.

what are you looking for?

Once you have decided where you will keep your horse, you can set about choosing one. It is vital to match your size and weight to your mount. It is also important to have a clear idea of which aspects of riding appeal to you; this will have a major influence on the type of animal you require.

Size

Deciding what size of horse to buy is particularly difficult with children, because they grow rapidly and soon become too big to ride a pony. You are then faced with deciding what to do with an animal that has been outgrown by its

Your choice of mount will be influenced by the size of the rider and what he or she is seeking to do with the horse. Sadly, ponies can soon be outgrown.

rider, but is a treasured friend. It is not fair to allow a child to continue riding an outgrown pony, which may cause lasting injury to the animal. To avoid having to pay for the upkeep of both the old pony and the new horse, you may want to defer any purchase until your child is older.

When choosing a pony for a child, those under 12.2hh will be suitable for children under 12 years old; ponies with a height between 12.2 and 13.2hh are recommended for riders aged between 12 and 14, while those up to a hand taller will suffice for most young riders over the course of the next two years. It is always better to obtain a slightly larger pony than you need; obviously, this is particularly recommended in the case of a child who is above average size.

Although the height of the horse is important when assessing its suitability for an adult, build is also a factor, with cobs, for example, being relatively strong for their size. The size of the mount is affected by the weight as well as the height of an adult, particularly as the weight of adults of the same size can vary quite widely. In general terms, a height from 15.2hh upward is suitable for most women, whereas for men, a horse above 16hh is likely to be best.

Breed

Those with a particular interest in breeding are most likely to seek purebred mares. Many of the horses offered for normal riding purposes are not of purebred stock, but are the result of a mating between a purebred stallion and a crossbred mare. This type of mixed breeding is preferred, since the stallion has a greater impact on the progeny under these circumstances, influencing aspects such as stamina and size. By changing the breed of stallion, a crossbred mare can be used to produce different types of

Cob is a description that is applied to a general type of horse, as well as to specific breeds, such as the Welsh cob. Cobs are steady and dependable by nature.

geldings. They may undergo slight shifts in temperament when they come into season, although this is only likely to be a problem during the spring and summer.

Buying a stallion is not a practical proposition for most people. They are usually kept only for stud purposes. A gelding is a male horse that has been neutered. Neutering makes the horse much more manageable, although, of course, there is no possibility of breeding with a gelding.

foals. Larger breeds, such as Hanoverians, will inevitably result in stockier offspring than, for example, Thoroughbreds, which are bred for their pace.

The horse's immediate ancestry can also affect its relative hardiness and, therefore, requirements for winter care. Those originating from warmer parts of the world, such as stock of Arab descent, are less hardy than breeds that evolved in more temperate climates—crossbred ponies, for example. In any case, ponies are generally hardier than horses. Pure pony breeds are usually very wellsuited to living outside for most of the year, so they rarely need stabling. This applies particularly to those, such as Shetlands or Welsh Mountain stock, that have adapted to survive in fairly harsh natural conditions.

Gender

Many people prefer mares, partly because if they are very successful in a discipline or have to be retired prematurely, there is the possibility of breeding from them. Some owners also consider mares are more amenable than

Age

The age of the horse will affect its price and its abilities. An unproven youngster is likely to be significantly cheaper than a horse that has won competitions. If you are considering buying a horse that is claimed to be a prize winner, it is worth checking its performance in show reports in equine magazines or with the relevant organization concerned, such as the national show jumping association. There can be advantages to buying a foal, but this is a serious undertaking since it will need to be taught everything from scratch (see pp.68–69 and 150–151).

The best type of horse for a novice is described as a schoolmaster. This is a horse of around eight years old, with experience in the discipline that interests you. A schoolmaster can be especially valuable if you are looking for a horse that jumps well. This is a skill that needs refining, so choosing a horse that is used to jumping should give you confidence as well.

A schoolmaster is often to be recommended when you are seeking your first horse.

what do you want to do?

One of the major factors influencing your choice of horse will be if and how you intend to compete. Bear this in mind at the outset, since some horses are more suitable for certain tasks than others. Lipizzaner horses, for example, have a particular talent for dressage, whereas in showing classes, conformation of the horse is especially significant. Select carefully; any basic deficiencies will be impossible to correct.

Showing

Showing is a popular pastime, with judges concentrating on the appearance or "type" of the entrants in each class, those corresponding most closely to the ideal being judged the winners. Horses or ponies are suitable for showing classes, with good behavior and conformation being two of the most important characteristics. If you are keen on showing, it is best to opt for a particular breed or type, which can then be entered in classes aimed specifically for it.

Show jumping

Show jumping is very popular, with classes at various levels, from local shows to national competitions. At the top levels, it requires excellent training and a high degree of skill, as well as corresponding fitness.

Successful show jumping entails competing against the clock, without incurring penalties.

Dressage

Dressage is less flamboyant, but exceptional understanding is required between horse and rider to be successful at this discipline, and training is a slow process. It takes at least four years of intensive training for a horse to approach Olympic standards, for example.

Eventing

Dressage and show jumping are two components that feature as part of eventing competitions. The third component is the cross-country section, in which horses jump a course that uses the natural terrain of the countryside. Steeplechasing and roadwork may also be included. Eventing, therefore, represents probably the most demanding challenge for horse and rider alike.

Western riding began and remains very popular in North America. It has its own design of tack and riders often wear the traditional stetson.

Endurance

Endurance riding is not for the fainthearted, being probably the ultimate test of both the horse and rider's fitness, with courses being up to 100 miles (161km) long. It has a very strong following in North America.

Sidesaddle

It used to be considered inappropriate for women to ride astride a horse, so they rode in this fashion, using a special

TOP LEFT: Dressage competitions are based on the ability of horse and rider to work together, carrying out a precise series of movements on which they are judged.

LEFT: Regular veterinary and blacksmith checks are carried out at stages when horses are participating in endurance races, to safeguard their welfare. Endurance horses may have log books detailing their past history.

BELOW: Gymkhanas test the abilities and agility of young riders, and can encourage them to participate in other disciplines in due course, once they have mastered the basics of riding.

saddle devised over 700 years ago. Riding sidesaddle is still popular today, with the fitting of the saddle being critical to prevent any spinal injury to the horse.

Western riding

There are a number of different styles of western riding, based on the western saddle (see p.123). The saddle's large and comfortable design derives from that of the Spanish saddles introduced to North America with horses in the 1500s, and its most noticeable feature is the raised pommel.

Riding Clubs

When they are starting to ride, many young people join the Pony Club. Established in Britain in 1929, it has grown into an international organization with branches in many countries, including the U.S.A. and Canada, as well as Australia and New Zealand. One of the most popular Pony Club activities is the gymkhana (derived from the Hindustani *gend-khana*—sports ground). A gymkhana offers a wide range of competitions that often involve racing against the clock. Ponies are better suited to this type of activity than horses, because they are more agile, even when they have only a moderate level of fitness.

finding
a horse

Once you have decided on the type of horse you are seeking and have set yourself a realistic budget, you can begin looking. Start by reading specialized equestrian magazines, many of which carry advertisements offering horses for sale. This will give you an idea of the horses on offer and, perhaps more importantly, an indication of their price. Always be particularly suspicious of horses that appear to be priced cheaply—they could have either chronic health or behavioral problems, or both. Never rush into a purchase on these grounds; it is likely to be a costly undertaking.

Why is the horse being sold?

Try to establish whether the person offering the horse has a genuine reason for wanting to sell it, which will suggest that it is not being sold because of some unpleasant vice. It might be a child's pony that has been outgrown, for example, or perhaps a change in job means the current owner no longer has time to spend with the horse. It helps if someone in your locality has an animal they want to sell, since you may be able to find out about its background more easily. If it has been a regular participant at shows or other events, you may even have friends who recollect seeing it in action.

Dear Equine Casebook

I recently visited an auction, where there were quite a few nice-looking horses being sold very cheaply. Is this a good way to buy a horse?
Sincerely, Jeremy Barton

If you are looking for your first horse, it is not wise to buy it at an auction. You really do need to have considerable experience before making a safe purchase at such sales. Even with experience, it is still possible to make a bad choice, partly because it is difficult to check up on the horse's background, whether it has chronic health problems or tendon injuries, for example. At auctions, horses are sold basically as seen, with no reliable safeguards.

Veterinary Inspection

When you think you have found your ideal horse, under normal circumstances and prior to completing the purchase, you should ask the seller if they have any objection to a veterinary inspection being carried out. This is a routine practice, so if they refuse, you should abandon your interest in that particular horse. Vetting entails the horse being given a standard examination by your vet, with any problems being noted in the resulting report. This process should detect any signs of lameness, past injuries, or underlying illness, such as respiratory disease, which could affect a horse's performance and may not be immediately obvious, particularly to a novice. It is clearly not possible for a vet to detect an illness that may not be showing obvious symptoms at the time of inspection, but it is certainly worth paying for vetting to be carried out. Otherwise, you could end up later not just with large veterinary bills, but also with an unsuitable horse.

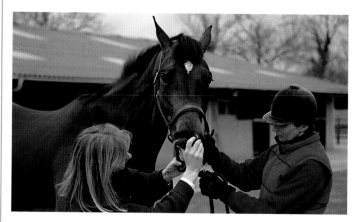

One of the first things that needs to be checked is the horse's age. This can be assessed by an examination of its teeth (see p.38). It is also worth noting how readily the horse cooperates in letting the vet inspect its mouth.

Dealers

When you contact a seller in response to an advertisement, try to find out as much as possible about the horse. Unfortunately, it is not unknown for some unscrupulous dealers to advertise as private individuals. There is an easy way to find out whether this is the case. When you first get in contact, say you are interested in the horse being advertised. If the seller has to ask you which one, you know they have more than one available and thus could be a dealer. Since this fact has not been made obvious at the outset, proceed with great caution.

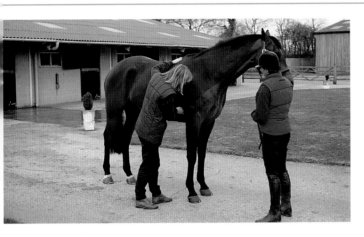

Using a stethoscope enables the vet to listen not just to the horse's heart, to detect any abnormalities there, but also to the lungs. Any damage to these will seriously compromise its performance.

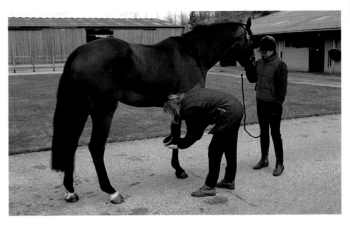

Soundness is obviously vital, and a close inspection of the lower limbs and feet forms a very important part of a veterinary inspection. It will be possible to detect signs of diseases such as laminitis (see p.40) as a result.

The way in which a horse moves can also help to reveal problems associated with its gait, and by trotting it vigorously your vet will then be able to listen to the airways again, comparing the results with those taken when the horse was at rest.

Flexion of the joints is a routine part of an inspection, but if there is a particular joint worry, an X-ray examination may be needed, using portable equipment, to ascertain the full extent of the problem.

There are, however, reputable professional dealers who buy and sell horses on a regular basis. Placing your trust in someone like this is not necessarily a bad idea, because they depend on satisfied customers to stay in business and will have built up a network of reliable contacts. If you do decide to buy through a dealer, for added insurance, seek someone who has been established for a long time and has built up a reputation, and make sure you prepare a detailed list of all your requirements before they start to look for an animal for you. When they do find you a horse, try it out carefully, and do not feel that you have to buy.

Insurance

You will need to think about insuring your horse after you have acquired it, and it is useful to have taken the time to investigate the various options beforehand. You can then take out the policy at soon as you have completed the purchase. Third-party insurance, to protect you in the event of your horse causing an accident, is essential for all horse owners. As far as the horse's health is concerned, bear in mind that in strange surroundings, with a new rider, this is the time when the horse is most likely to become ill or injure itself (see p.74).

conformation

Being able to assess a horse's conformation, basically its proportions, is very important when it comes to deciding on its suitability for particular tasks, and can also indicate likely problems, such as a tendency to stumble. You may blame the horse because it proves to be a clumsy jumper, but this could be more a fault of its conformation, which causes it to drag its feet, than any reflection of its character. The different breeds each have a distinctive build, and the shape of a horse's body can also change with age. Old horses are often described as hollow-backed, thanks to the dip that develops in this part of the body as they age.

Head

The shape of a horse's head is popularly supposed to provide an insight into its temperament. Those with small eyes in comparison with their head are reputedly ill-natured, while a horse that puts its ears back when approached is thought to be bad-tempered and difficult to deal with. Horses with fairly broad heads are considered to have a better disposition than those with a more elegant shape.

Neck

The size and shape of the neck may have a distinct impact on the ease with which a horse can be ridden. Concavity along the top of the neckline, known as "ewe" neck, is considered a weakness. Here, the underside of the neck is more heavily muscled and protrudes, which can make riding difficult in extreme cases, simply because the bridle will not fit well and the saddle may tend to slip forward.

The Perfectly Proportioned Horse

There is no such thing as a standard conformation in the case of horses, because the shape of their bodies—or conformation—is directly influenced by the purpose for which they are bred. The relative proportions of the body are significant, with a heavy, thick-set frame revealing a horse bred for power and strength.

A horse bred for speed has a lighter body and longer legs. It is the way in which the proportions come together that influences the conformation. The proportions of the body in various respects are of common length, in cases of good conformation, as shown in the accompanying diagram (middle right).

Good conformation means the horse can carry out its work effectively.

LEFT: The conformation of the head varies between individuals. Some have a straight head, while those of Arab descent have a noticeably dished profile.

Chest and front legs

The chest should be broad and deep, to provide good lung capacity. If it is very narrow, the horse may have to wear a breast plate, to prevent the saddle from slipping. In extreme cases, the inner faces of the front legs will be very close together, which will affect the horse's movement. The conformation of the front legs is very important. Ideally, there should be a straight line extending down from the shoulder passing through the center of the knee and both the fetlock and foot. Recognized deviations include pigeon toes, caused by the fetlocks being turned in and putting strain on these joints.

Hindlimbs

Poor conformation is more common in the hindlimbs, but here the effects are less serious. Ideally, the end of the buttock muscle should form part of a straight line that extends down through the center of the hock, the fetlock, and foot, when the horse is viewed from behind. The conformation of the hock joint is especially important,

Feet

Fore foot 45°–50°
Hind foot 50°–55°

The conformation of the feet must not be overlooked, with the ideal being shown above. It is particularly important that the feet point forward in their pairs and show no signs of deviation. If they turn out, this is likely to cause brushing, which is when the feet come into contact with each other as the horse moves. Feet that turn inward from the midline can cause injury to the fetlock. The relationship between the hoof and pastern is especially significant as the horse moves. Long toes increase the likelihood of navicular disease.

because it is responsible for absorbing the concussive effect arising from movement. Horses with markedly angular hocks are at greater risk of suffering from a sprain of the plantar ligament, which runs down the back of the joint. Such an injury is known as a curb.

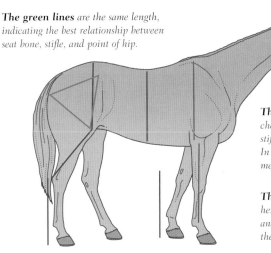

The green lines *are the same length, indicating the best relationship between seat bone, stifle, and point of hip.*

The blue lines *show head, girth, chestnut to foot, croup to stifle, stifle to hock, and hock to ground. In a perfect horse, all are the same measurement.*

The red lines *show that the height from the fetlock to the elbow and the distance from the withers to the elbow should be equal.*

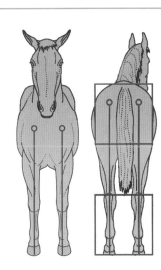

The purple lines *reveal the perfect relationship between the parts of a horse from the back and the front. On the left, the point of shoulder, knee, fetlock, and hoof should all be aligned. On the right, the seat bone lines up with the point of hock and the center of the fetlock and hoof. The measurement of each side of the two squares indicated should be exactly the same as that of the length of the head.*

considering **character**

When choosing a horse that is suitable for the work you want it to undertake, you should also take into consideration its temperament and breeding. Do not be guided simply by liking the appearance of a horse. Just because it has a good conformation, there are no guarantees that you will bond well together. Breeding, background, and health all have an effect on the temperament of a horse.

Breeding

There are distinctive differences in temperament, reflected by the breed background of an individual. Heavy horses are generally very phlegmatic characters, with patient natures, as are cobs. On the other hand, Arabs and Thoroughbreds tend to be highly strung, as befits their athletic natures. It can be very difficult to find suitable homes for racehorses after retirement simply because their highly strung temperaments require specialized management.

Experiences

Aside from breeding, much also depends on the horse's previous experiences, such as the way in which it has been treated and

Stable vices (see pp.156–159) will not necessarily be obvious when you are simply viewing a horse.

Vices and Behavioral Disorders

Spend time looking at the horse that you are thinking of acquiring, before even approaching it. You should then be able to gain some insight into its character, whether it is stabled or out in a field. Unfortunately, however, it can be quite difficult to detect certain vices on the basis of just a brief encounter of this type. You are less likely to be able to detect signs of crib sucking, for example, when the horse is out in a field, compared with when it is stabled. If you note anything that concerns you, ask the seller and draw it to the attention of the vet who is carrying out an inspection for you. While advertisements may give some reassurance regarding a horse's temperament, these are not warranties and should not be relied upon.

Although many horses will often become excited when they are first turned out, a horse that rears repeatedly in this way in a field is likely to prove very difficult to control and will not be a good choice.

Always seek the opportunity to ride the horse yourself. You need to be sure that a horse will be biddable, being willing to follow your instructions, such as riding across a stream if necessary.

trained. Very few horses are actually born with a nasty temperament, but they will acquire unpleasant traits from bad handling. This is why it is so important to check out the background of a horse prior to purchase, so you can be sure, as far as possible, that it has no bad vices (the box on p.64 gives some tips on how to spot these).

If you are used to a riding school mount, be prepared for a difference when assessing the temperament of a horse that has been kept privately. Riding school horses can become rather bored with following the same routine, and this often leads to them seeming very placid. However, the same horse, given a change of scenery, will often prove much more lively.

Health

The physical condition of a horse can have an effect on its temperament. One that is in a poor state, perhaps suffering from a heavy burden of parasites, is likely to be far less lively than if it was in good health. Similarly, a horse that has been stabled, with little opportunity for exercise, may become very excitable when allowed out and ridden. Bear this in mind if you are thinking of buying a horse whose present owner is having to sell through lack of time.

Dear Equine Casebook

I fell in love with a horse that seemed quiet and affectionate, but now I have got him home, he tries to bite me when I tack him up.
Best wishes, Lucy Walker

Do not despair. Your horse is still adjusting to a new home. With a little time and patience, it is possible to win the trust of even the most nervous individual, and in so doing, increase its capabilities. It is worth considering whether he

is in pain—not necessarily from something that is physically wrong, but simply because of badly fitting tack, such as a saddle or bridle. Do not assume that the tack he came with fits properly. Particularly suspect this type of problem if your horse appears to be cooperative in other ways. If you are in any doubt about his health, get him checked by a vet, and it is worth calling in your saddler to make sure his tack is not the problem.

going *through*
the paces

If you find a horse that seems suitable, it is advisable to see it go through its regular routine, which should highlight potential problems, such as whether it is reluctant to be caught in a field or is difficult to persuade into a horse trailer. A horse that is well schooled is likely to be a more reliable prospect than a badly trained animal, especially for the novice owner. It is also very useful to see the tack in which the horse is usually ridden, which may reveal much about possible problems associated with riding it. A standing martingale, for example, suggests that the horse may naturally attempt to keep its head too high.

The bridle and the bit, which fits into the horse's mouth, assist the rider in controlling the horse's movements. It is important to choose the right combination for an individual horse.

Trying Out the Horse

It is vital to ride any horse you are thinking of buying, both in the school and out on a hack, if possible. This will tell you a lot about it and whether you like the way it feels. Do not be surprised if it seems less responsive to you than it is with its regular rider; this need not be a cause for concern. But there are occasions when horses display a particular dislike for people of a certain gender, usually men, and the reason for this reaction probably resides in repeated mistreatment in the past, which it has not forgotten. This form of fear is very difficult to counter in many cases, especially since it can resurface when, for example, the farrier visits or a judge approaches in the show ring.

At walk

Watch the horse as it walks, from both front and back. Its movement should be smooth, with the joints being flexed as appropriate, to create an even gait. Should the horse be reluctant to flex its legs properly, it will tend to stumble, as well as covering only a relatively short distance at each stride. Pay particular attention to the feet because, even if the horse is not lame, conformation faults can be revealed through their action. In some cases, such faults can also be indicated by the wear on the shoes. If it is uneven, this may be due to a peculiarity in the gait. If there is heavy wear on the outer edge, for example, the horse may have an undesirable paddling gait, with the toe tending to move inward, toward the midline and then outward again, rather than progressing directly forward. The reverse of this problem, described as "dishing" or "winging," is caused by the toe being directed outward, and the wear in this case is on the inner side of the shoe.

Carry Out a Thorough Examination

When you find a horse that you like, do not be afraid to ask the seller to demonstate as many of its purported abilities as you want to see. It is vital that you are happy with a horse's behavior when it is being led, as well as its performance when it is being ridden. Watch, too, as it is being tacked up, to see whether there is any sign of resistance at any stage. For example, check if it seems to be reluctant to pick its feet up, if it pulls faces when it is being groomed, if it is unhappy about approaching a mounting block, or if it moves around restlessly once mounted. All these can be indicators of underlying problems, although they can also be caused by inexperience and so, with time and patience, may not be insurmountable.

When assessing a horse's soundness, you should see it being put through its paces, when any weakness is likely to show up. A smooth rhythm is obviously essential throughout the exercise.

As the horse passes you, you will have the benefit of seeing it trotting from different angles. If you are concerned about its gait, ask for the horse to be trotted back past you in the other direction.

You may be able to pick up other indicators regarding its temperament as well. A nervous individual may be reluctant to continue trotting once it is expected to move out from the confines of the yard.

Ask any questions you need to. Depending on the circumstances, some of the horse's tack may be for sale, so make suitable inquiries and inspections to ascertain condition and fit.

Watching the horse being ridden is essential, and riding it yourself is also to be recommended, to help you to pick up any behavioral quirks. Remember the horse may not be used to being ridden by a stranger.

Watch out for just how biddable a horse is. It should be quite easy to persuade it to progress from a trot to a canter. You will be able to feel any problems with the gait when you ride the horse yourself.

At trot

You are more likely to spot signs of lameness when the horse is being trotted. This is because it will be harder for the horse to conceal the sensitivity of the foot, or the problem affecting its leg, at a faster speed. Your vet will also be able to assess the overall level of fitness, having checked the horse over when it was at rest, by examining it again after a period of exercise.

At canter

Encouraging the horse to canter in a circle will clearly show how well it lifts its legs, and this movement has the added advantage of determining the degree of suppleness in the horse's back. Persuading it to move in an ever tighter circle, both clockwise and counterclockwise, serves to show that it can cross its hind legs without difficulty. Watch again for any sign of unsoundness.

buying
a foal

Although there can be advantages to buying a foal, not the least of which is that it should not have developed serious vices at a young age, there are drawbacks as well, particularly if you have little experience. You will need to train the young horse to be ridden and then teach it the discipline you are interested in. All this will take a great deal of time, although if you are fortunate enough to have experienced advice to guide you, it can be immensely rewarding.

You will also have to be patient, since young horses may not be broken until they are four years old. In addition, there are no guarantees about the ability of the horse, even if it is bred from a good bloodline. This is made abundantly clear by the racing industry, where promising youngsters frequently fail to make the grade. Foals are naturally quite playful and high-spirited, so it is important that the young horse is used to walking on a headcollar (see p.131); otherwise, it will be very difficult to handle. You will obviously not be able to determine its suitability for riding at this stage, but it is important to pay particular attention to its conformation for this reason.

Settling it in

The first difficulty you are likely to face on bringing your foal home is being able to settle it down in the absence of its mother. Horses tend not to thrive when they are kept by themselves and this certainly applies to youngsters. It may be advantageous to obtain a much older

To prevent weaning difficulties, a foal must not only be kept out of sight, but also out of sound of its mother when they are first separated.

Reasons Not to Buy a Foal

Buying a foal is a serious, long-term commitment, and you should be prepared to consider all the disadvantages beforehand. Long before you can ride your youngster, the costs will continue to mount up in terms of food and bedding, blacksmith charges, and routine health care, with colts having to be gelded as yearlings. The youngster's feet will need to be checked and trimmed back as necessary, roughly every six weeks on average, and certainly in the early days it will be important to keep a check on the weight of the foal by weighing it regularly. As the young horse develops, there is always the risk that it will not meet your requirements, and deficiencies in its conformation may become apparent. Bear in mind that foals do not grow evenly, but in spurts, so it can be quite difficult to spot the true potential of an individual, especially if you do not have much experience of judging young horses.

It is very important that a foal learns to be led from an early age, partly because a young horse is relatively easy to manage at this stage, thanks to its size.

animal on loan as a companion, but you need to agree in writing what you are liable for if the horse becomes ill in your care. Never be tempted to keep a donkey as a companion, because they carry lungworms and there is the risk that your horse will become infested.

If you buy a foal that has just been weaned, find out the diet it has been receiving and stick to this as closely as possible to minimize the risk of any digestive upset. You will need to be prepared to keep the foal boxed for at least two weeks, so you can keep a check on its wellbeing. Then, assuming the weather is good, you can allow it out into a secure paddock during the day, bringing it back in again at night. At first it may be rather nervous, which is where an older companion can be of assistance. During the summer, it should then be possible to allow the foal to stay out permanently. It may be able to remain in its field over the following winter, provided it has a suitable shelter.

You must be prepared to lead the foal every day using a halter, so that you continue to be able to control it as it matures into a larger adult.

Making Early Progress

Once your foal is two or three years old, it may benefit from some light work to get it used to being handled and to build up its muscles. Do not overdo this activity, however, as it is easy to make a youngster stale.

Lungeing a youngster will teach obedience to the aids (see p.139) and begins work toward an acceptance of the saddle and bridle, as well as being ridden, in due course. The horse will also establish a bond with you through this regular exercise.

You may find that when being lunged, your horse will at first try to pull away or may slow down rather than progressing at the pace you want. Gentle encouragement from a lungeing whip is sometimes required.

You will be able to assess your horse's gait by lungeing it regularly. Do not be afraid to use your voice as a way to communicate with your horse at this stage, since it is a useful training tool that you will use when riding.

Exercise is important to keep a young horse not just physically fit, but also mentally alert. Try to vary the routine to an extent so your horse does not become bored. A bored horse is more likely to play up.

getting your
horse home

It is very important that your horse will travel without difficulty in a trailer, because not only do you have to have it brought home, but there will inevitably be other times when it needs to be moved, not least to events. The seller may be prepared to deliver the horse to you or, for an appropriate fee based on the distance, you may be able to arrange for someone with a trailer to pick it up for you.

Traveling equipment

You will need to buy or borrow the necessary equipment to make sure your horse travels safely. Leg protectors are vital to protect against possible injury to the limbs, should the horse slip on its journey. Either use the leg guards made specifically for the purpose or wrap traveling bandages around the lower part of the legs, extending from beneath the knees and hocks down to the coronet. Knee and hock boots are also to be recommended, while extra protection

TRAVELING

Even if you do not intend to compete with your horse regularly, it is vital that it is trained to be easily transported. Otherwise, it can not only be inconvenient and embarrassing, but also dangerous.

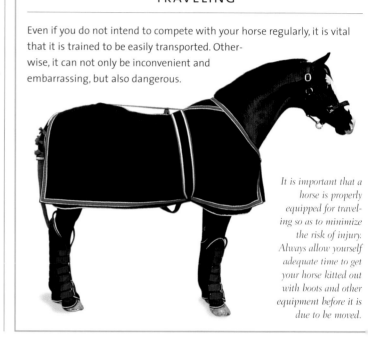

It is important that a horse is properly equipped for traveling so as to minimize the risk of injury. Always allow yourself adequate time to get your horse kitted out with boots and other equipment before it is due to be moved.

Dear Equine Casebook

I recently bought a young horse, and it took us five hours to get it into the trailer to bring it home. I am now worried that the next time I need to take it anywhere I will have the same problem, which could be embarrassing, particularly at a showground.
Yours sincerely, Margaret Short

A young horse that is unfamiliar with a trailer will be difficult to transport. This is why it is important to train youngsters to load as a matter of course, before you need to move them anywhere. This way, they can get used to the procedure. Don't worry. With a little patience, you can overcome most loading problems. Horses can often be reluctant to enter such a confined space at first, so use plenty of words of encouragement and consider feeding a tidbit. Park the trailer in a safe location and then lead the horse up the ramp, using a bridle to give a greater degree of control if it appears to be reluctant. Always try to encourage it to enter the box voluntarily rather than trying to force it. Should the horse walk a short distance up the ramp and then stop, you may be able to persuade it to advance by lifting each foreleg in turn, placing them progressively farther up the ramp. Alternatively, keep walking the horse up and down the ramp so that ultimately, it becomes possible to lead it into the box itself. Provide a hay net inside, and leave the horse tied up there for short periods. When used around the hindquarters, lungeing reins can sometimes be successful in persuading the horse to enter.

A side-opening horse trailer is just one variation on horse transportation. The horse should be happy to follow you up the ramp without rushing. This one looks somewhat tense about entering. It could do with some time and practice.

As you reach the ramp top, steady the horse to enter the box. Be careful that it does not try to back off again. Ideally, there should be longer side gates here, as a panicking horse might get its legs caught between these and the ramp.

in the form of coronet boots may be advisable for longer journeys. A tail bandage is also important, particularly when a horse is being moved in a trailer, since it will tend to lean back against the tailgate, and an uprotected tail will get rubbed and damaged as a result.

Do not forget to put on a traveling blanket to make sure your horse does not get too cold, or that if it gets hot, it does not chill on cooling down.

Comfort

Providing a hay net often encourages a horse to settle down. If the journey is likely to last for more than a few hours, be prepared to stop and allow it an opportunity to drink. Since horses are unable to vomit, because of the structure of their palate, and appear to be immune to travel sickness, there is no need to worry that horses will get sick, but they often get hot in the confines of the trailer, so ventilation is very important. Finally, remember to tie the horse up once it is securely confined.

Many trailers are designed so the box is very low to the ground and there is no ramp. Horses are taught to step up into the box and seem happy to do so.

settling in
to a new home

When moving a horse to new stables, be sure that everything is prepared well in advance before your arrival, so your horse can be transferred to its new quarters at once. Here, a straw bed is being made ready.

Prepare your new horse's stable before you set out to bring it home. Then, when you arrive, you can simply unload it and lead it directly into its new quarters. Bear in mind that the change in environment will be a very stressful period for the horse, and it should be allowed to settle down for a day or so in its new surroundings. This is a good time to organize such things as a visit from the blacksmith and the equine dentist, and getting vaccinations done.

Once your horse has made itself at home, you can start working together to build up a bond. Spend time each day just observing it, whether it is in a stable or out at grass, so you can become familiar with its behavior. This will have the advantage of alerting you at an early stage if it becomes ill or starts to display signs of lameness.

Unloading your Horse

Although it can be difficult to persuade a horse to enter a trailer up a ramp, it is equally important that a horse will walk safely out of the box down the ramp when it arrives at its destination. Some may instead rear up or rush out quickly from the confinement of the box. If possible, have a few practices with your horse before you finally pick it up. Bear in mind, however, that after the unfamiliar sensations of the journey, your horse is likely to be rather stressed and may not behave as well as during its previous training sessions.

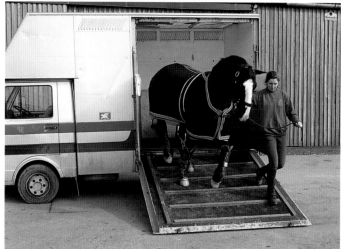

Getting your priorities right

Unless you were handed the vaccination certificates by the horse's previous owner, there is no guarantee that the important immunizations against tetanus and influenza are up-to-date. These should be arranged as a priority, because such illnesses are serious. Should a horse become ill, it may not recover, and if it does, its performance may be compromised in any case. If you have not taken out an insurance policy on your horse before bringing it home, now is the time to do so.

Both you and your horse will need to get used to the stable routine at a new yard. Horses invariably take an interest in what is going on around them, watching what is happening even though they may not be involved.

Tetanus

Horses are very susceptible to the effects of the toxin produced by the bacterium known as *Clostridium tetani*. The clostridial bacteria responsible are found in soil and can be introduced to the body through wounds, particularly deep puncture wounds, where they thrive, releasing a deadly nerve toxin. Stiffness of the muscles involved in

What is equine influenza and how important is it that I protect my horse against it? Friends say that it's not always necessary to inject, but I want to be sure that I do the right thing for my new horse.

Sincerely, John Peterson

There are two main strains of equine influenza, and the illness is passed on very rapidly between unvaccinated individuals, being spread by sneezing and by contact with nasal discharges. The incubation period is very short, typically between one and three days, so an epidemic can develop very quickly in a stable. In mild cases, horses take two or three weeks to recover, but often the period is much longer and can extend over six months, during which time there is always the risk of complications, such as secondary bacterial infections leading to pneumonia. Although equine flu is usually not fatal, it can cause lasting damage to the respiratory system.

All horses need to be protected against equine influenza by vaccination, since there is no effective treatment for this viral disease. Although it will not offer complete protection, if your horse contracts the virus, the resulting illness should be shorter and less severe. Two doses need to be given initially, separated by a gap of about six weeks, with a third dose after six months. Annual boosters to maintain immunity are then necessary, although if there is an outbreak in the area, an earlier booster may be advised by your vet. The immunization program in foals can begin as soon as they are three months old.

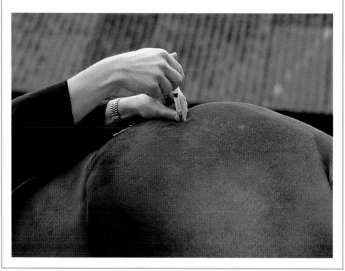

chewing is typical, which is why the disease is also known as lockjaw. Other symptoms include the appearance of the so-called third eyelid at the corner of each eye, muscular spasms of the neck and back, and a stiff, extended tail.

Two vaccines, given six weeks apart, followed by an annual booster will safeguard your horse against the effects of tetanus, which are frequently fatal. Once symptoms develop, treatment is difficult, and even if the horse survives, it will almost certainly be vulnerable to tetanus in the future if it is not vaccinated.

Tetanus is especially common in some areas of the world, and vaccination of pregnant mares in the last six weeks of pregnancy is one means of providing some protection for their foals after birth.

Insurance

Your insurance policy needs to cover your horse—against illness, loss, and theft—and yourself. First, compare as many different policies as possible to be sure that you select the one most suitable for your circumstances. Note particularly the amount of veterinary cover that is provided, because surgery on horses, for colic for example, can be very expensive. If you buy a young horse that starts to win prizes and so increases in value, do not forget to tell the insurance company and increase the premiums accordingly, since payments are otherwise likely to be scaled down in the event of a claim.

Many policies also provide ancillary protection against the theft of tack or your trailer. This is well worth considering. All horse owners must have cover for public liability, which you will need in the event of an accident occurring between you and your horse and a third party. Personal accident insurance is advisable—you will be thankful for it if you are injured in a fall from your horse.

The other risks that you should insure against are theft and straying. The latter can happen, especially if your horse is kept at grass. Although such cover cannot replace your horse, it does mean that you can acquire another, which might not otherwise be a financial possibility.

Identification

Even if your horse is fully insured, you obviously do not want to go through the upsetting experience of having it stolen. There are a number of steps you can take to safeguard it from becoming the target of thieves. The most notable of these is to get a freeze brand, which is very obvious and cannot be easily obscured (see box, right).

Most horses have unique markings on their coats, which can also be used for identification purposes, particularly if there is a dispute over ownership. These include facial markings, such as white blazes or stars, and leg markings, such as socks or white stripes on the feet. Other distinctive features are whorls of hair on various parts of the body and any nicks or scars. These may have been noted down during your horse's vetting (see pp.60–61), but it is a good idea also to photograph or video your horse to show these features, as well as recording them clearly on a chart.

Other methods of identification, such as hoof branding, can be helpful, but they are not permanent, with hoof branding typically lasting just six months. Also, such methods may not be visible enough to act as a deterrent to a thief. Microchipping is not visible, but does enable the owner of a stolen horse to be traced. This technique entails the injection of a small microchip in the neck. The microchip has a unique code, logged on a central database at the time of the implant. It can be read by a special scanner passed over it. This hiddens means of identification can be vital if your horse is recovered.

Freeze-branding

The technique, which is painless, entails freezing a code on a pigmented area of the coat (the branding iron is chilled to minus 293°C in liquid nitrogen). This kills the pigment cells, so the hair turns white, highlighting the code, which will remain permanently visible for the rest of the horse's life.

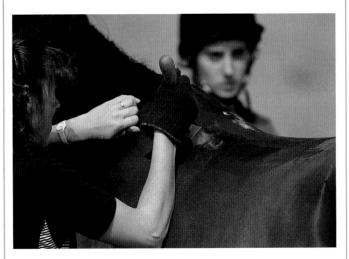

Usually the area just behind the shoulder is used for branding, although the shoulder itself is sometimes branded. It is important that your horse stands still during this process so a clear impression can be created.

Freeze-branding results in a permanent mark, which is recorded in a central database. This then acts as a discouragement to thieves who may be hoping to steal your horse to sell it.

introducing
horses to each other

After a move, your horse is likely to be stabled alongside other horses that it has not met before, and it may be turned out in the field with some of them. Although horses are sociable by nature, a group will have established hierarchies; introducing a newcomer can cause a breakdown of these and may lead to displays of aggression. By being careful about how you make introductions, however, it is possible to minimize the risk of conflict. It helps if your new horse has an opportunity to see and meet some of the others individually, without any group pressure, away from the stable, on a hack, for example.

When turning a horse out in a field for the first time, it is not a good idea simply to put it in with the others. Instead, start by placing the new arrival with a horse that is known to be placid. Put these two in a paddock that adjoins the one with the main group, so all the horses can see and make contact with each other over the fence. When the two horses are settled, you can begin to move

Dear Equine Casebook

I have a lovely horse that I have owned for about ten years. He is nearing retirement, so I recently bought a youngster to ride. My old horse has always been good natured and gentle, but he seems to have taken against the new one and drives her away every time I go into the field to catch her. He has also become difficult at mealtimes, lunging and biting at my youngster. Can you help?

Worried owner, Annabel Andrews

It is possible for a horse to become jealous of a new companion, and this problem is often created when, as you describe, an owner acquires a second horse to be kept at grass with their established mount. Although the initial introduction may be fine, friction is generated by the fact that, in an attempt to settle the newcomer and to win its confidence, the owner spends more time with this horse, excluding the first horse. This horse then reacts aggressively to what is perceived as a challenge to its relationship with its owner. You can prevent this problem from arising very easily, simply by giving more attention to the first horse, so the new arrival accepts a subservient role from the outset. You may be able to correct a conflict of this type by acknowledging the dominant individual first.

Horses display strong herd instincts, and individuals in a group can form close bonds.

If two horses have a strong bond, there can be difficulties when one is removed for a while, then reintroduced. There is unlikely to be any problem after a short separation, but a separation over several weeks or more may be more problematic. The risk will be reduced if the horses are in a herd rather than a pair, as there is less potential for constant bullying.

Always keep a close watch when introducing horses to each other. It is much better to turn them both out together at the same time, rather than bringing a new horse into a field that already has a resident.

other docile horses into their field. Each time, allow things to settle down again, keeping a close watch on any adverse reactions. It is important that there is plenty of space in the field and that the grazing is good since both these factors will lessen the pressure. Horses can be very territorial if food is scarce, so if there is little grazing, the established herd members will be more inclined to drive the newcomer away, rather than accept it into their midst.

There is unlikely to be instant harmony, but there should be no major signs of disagreement—any serious display of aggression could leave one or more of the group badly injured. It is much better to progress slowly rather than being faced with a full-scale conflict where the combatants need to be separated, and there is a much reduced likelihood of being able to reintroduce them successfully in the future. Once a bond has been formed, there is unlikely to be discord when the group is reunited after separation—if one member is taken out for a day to go to a show, for example. On the other hand, once two horses have taken a dislike to each other, there is little that can be done to reconcile the differences between them.

getting your horse
fit for work

When you acquire a new horse, you may need to work on its fitness, just as you would have to do if you had an animal recuperating after an injury or illness. You must also always allow plenty of time to prepare for a particular competition or event. Expecting too much of your horse, too soon, can easily lead to it breaking down and suffering a long lay-off. Avoid rushing through any fitness program and do not forget to increase the horse's food intake in accordance with its work rate. While you are exercising it, keep a watch on your horse's breathing rate. If it becomes noticeably out of breath and does not return to normal soon after the exercise has stopped, you are pushing it too hard.

Beginnings

Start off by walking your horse on a hard surface on a regular basis. Roadwork is often recommended, but this depends on how busy the roads are and how your horse reacts to traffic. Keep a check on its shoes, which will be more susceptible to wear during roadwork. It is also advisable to use knee boots, particularly with inexperienced horses.

Exposure to firm ground is very important in toning up the ligaments and tendons, as well as the muscles. Provided you make sure your horse moves at a reasonable pace, there will be cardiovascular benefits, too. It can take three weeks of such exercise, starting off at about 30 minutes daily, and increasing to 90 minutes, to build up the fitness of a hunter, while racehorses may need six weeks to get into shape.

Building up

The next stage is to introduce short periods of trotting, allowing the horse to trot for roughly a minute, about four times during the course of its 90-minute exercise regime. You can then extend the length of the trotting periods, and make them harder by going up short and then longer hills.

At this stage, it is a good idea to switch to firm ground, where there are no ruts, because an asphalt surface can become too hard on the joints.

Moving on

Three weeks of fairly disciplined trotting should result in a noticeable improvement in your horse's fitness. The next stage is to start cantering, taking care to warm up properly beforehand to minimize the risk of injury.

Depending on progress, you can then take the horse up gradually through its paces from a walk to a gallop and slow it down again. Schooling exercises may be introduced, too. The actual length of the training sessions is still about 90 minutes or so, but their intensity will have increased noticeably.

Fitness is something that is built up gradually and should not be rushed, lest this increases the risk of injury. At the outset, ascertaining the amount of work to which a new horse has been accustomed can be helpful.

ABOVE: *Gentle roadwork of this type can be a valuable way of increasing a horse's level of fitness after a layoff, but choose your location carefully so there will be minimal passing traffic and good visibility.*

BELOW: *Horses often become excited when they are first turned out in a field, and this opportunity for exercise will increase their level of activity and thus their fitness. It is vital to check first that the fencing is secure.*

Swimming as Therapy

Horses are able to swim surprisingly well, with their powerful legs enabling them to swim quite strongly when in deep water. This means they can ford rivers and has also at times allowed them to escape from flooded pastures.

Over recent years the therapeutic advantages of swimming have become appreciated, and there are now centers where horses—especially valuable competition horses such as racehorses—are encouraged to swim in special pools under supervision. This helps them to retain their fitness when recuperating from an injury, particularly one that restricts the ability of their limbs to take their weight. Most horses react well to being introduced to swimming facilities of this type, especially under the guidance of an experienced handler. Equine health insurance may cover the costs involved if your vet feels that your horse could benefit from this type of therapy.

Rest days

Throughout this fitness training, always allow the horse to rest for one day of the week. On its day off, it should be let out of its stable for a lengthy period of grazing if at all possible. This will prevent stiffness from developing, as horses move around more in a field than when confined.

establishing a partnership

3

By evolving a stimulating routine for your horse, you will establish a good relationship with it and reduce the likelihood of behavioral difficulties. It is vital that you learn to recognize when your horse is off-color, which will enable you to seek veterinary advice at an early stage, which, in turn, means the problem can hopefully be resolved without becoming major or even life-threatening. Remember that horses can never be entirely predictable, and always allow for the unexpected when you introduce yours to something new: clipping it for the first time, for example. If you encounter abnormal behavior in your horse, try to resolve it as soon as possible. Never be afraid to ask for help. In larger yards, you may even find someone who has had a similar experience.

looking after your horse's feet

The care of a horse's feet is a very important aspect of its daily management. From the outset you will need to be able to pick up each foot in turn. Always choose a quiet spot in the yard or field to do this, so that your horse will not be upset by any disturbance. Initially, it may help to have someone hold your horse while you pick its feet up, but once a routine is established, you should be able to pick them up while it is tied up.

The procedure

Never be tempted to bend down and lift the foot without warning, especially with a newly acquired horse. Instead, approach slowly and run your hand gently down its leg, speaking softly to reassure it if it appears to be nervous. Once you reach the foot, lean gently against the horse, which should make it shift its weight onto the other side of its body. This will allow you to lift its leg more easily. Take particular care with the hind legs, being careful not to stand behind the horse, where you could be kicked, and do not forget the horse's blind spot (see p.31) around its rump when approaching from the side.

The underside of the feet need to be cleaned regularly using a hoof pick. Always work in a downward movement, from the heel to the toe, to avoid damaging the heel and frog at the back of the hoof (see p.85). The frog is especially important, because it makes initial contact with the ground and serves to prevent the horse from slipping, as well as helping to absorb the force of movement. If the underside, or sole, of the hoof suffers any damage, it can extend to other structures deeper within the foot, which may lead to lameness or other complications.

Trimming and shoeing

Even if its shoes are not very worn, your horse is likely to need to see the blacksmith every month or so to have its feet trimmed; the horn covering at the front of the hoof is usually particularly in need of attention. Horses at grass and not being ridden also need attention from the blacksmith. Even ponies, which are less commonly shod, even when working, need to have their feet trimmed regularly.

Having removed the old shoe, the blacksmith will pare back the horn. He will then prepare a new shoe, if required, fitting it carefully to the hoof while it is still hot, before cooling it in water and then nailing it in place. Special nails are used for this purpose and should keep the shoe firmly secured as it wears down. Protruding clips at the front of the shoe—usually one on each of the front shoes and two on the hinds—provide further support.

Horses need to have their feet attended to regularly to prevent lameness. Cleaning the feet is very important, while shoeing serves to protect the hooves from damage during work.

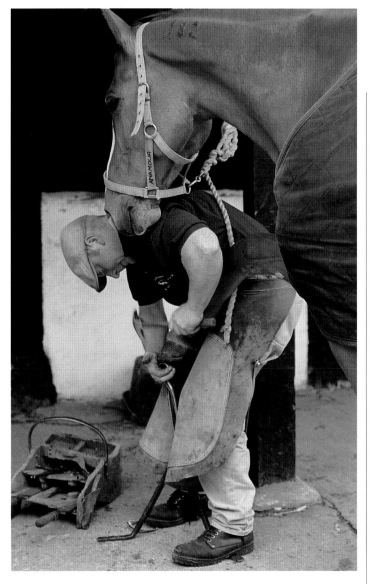

Regular visits from the blacksmith are vital to a horse's wellbeing, and the shoes will be made individually to conform to the needs of your horse.

Types of shoe

There are various types of shoe, such as those intended to give hunters extra grip, and your smith will chose the sort that is most suitable for the work your horse is currently doing. There are also surgical shoes (see box), which can help to compensate for deformities in the foot or faults in the horse's action. Studs may be recommended, if, for example, your horse is doing a lot of roadwork.

Remedial Shoes

In some cases, particularly when a horse may have a faulty action or is suffering from a weakness of the hoof, remedial shoes may be advised by the blacksmith. To reduce the risk of injuries caused by brushing, for example, when one leg is hit by its neighbor, either a feather-edged shoe or a three-quarters shoe may be recommended. Shoes with rolled toes will prevent overreaching injuries, when the hindlegs come into contact with the forelegs. Shoes may also be devised to help rest an injury. The Patten shoe has a raised heel and a bar, and is used for tendon injuries.

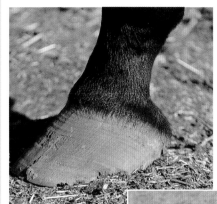

LEFT: If horses' hooves are neglected, they are likely to grow in an increasingly deformed way, and it will take time to get them sound again.

BELOW: This horse's neglected hoof has been partially rebuilt with plastic to protect it until it starts to grow again properly.

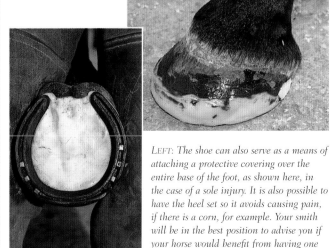

LEFT: The shoe can also serve as a means of attaching a protective covering over the entire base of the foot, as shown here, in the case of a sole injury. It is also possible to have the heel set so it avoids causing pain, if there is a corn, for example. Your smith will be in the best position to advise you if your horse would benefit from having one or more special shoes.

grooming
your horse

If you do not have one already, you will need to invest in a grooming kit, which is usually kept in a special carrying box (shown below). Your kit should include a body brush, which is used for general grooming, its soft bristles helping to remove dust. It is cleaned using a curry comb. A dandy

brush is needed to remove dried mud. Dandy brushes have hard bristles and must not be used on the mane or tail, because they will damage the longer hair, nor after clipping, or if the horse has very sensitive skin. Plastic or rubber curry combs are alternatives to the dandy brush. They also stimulate the skin and can help to improve the natural gloss on the coat. A similar effect can be obtained using a cactus cloth, especially if it is dampened slightly before use. This is basically a piece of sackcloth, and it can be used over the entire body.

A mane comb is useful as its deep teeth enable the long mane and tail hair to be groomed easily. For plaiting purposes (see p.90), a short comb is required.

You will also need a couple of water brushes: one is to clean the feet if they become very muddy; the other is dampened and used to remove dust from the coat. It is also useful for grooming the mane.

Wisps and stable cloths

Many horses enjoy being groomed with a wisp or leather massage pad, both of which can be used in conjunction with a stable cloth to improve the muscle tone. The wisp is made from plaited lengths of hay and should be dampened with a little water. The wisp or pad is applied firmly over the muscular areas of the horse's body, such as the hindquarters, causing it to tense its muscles, which are then relaxed with the stable rubber.

Sponges and sweat scrapers

Two sponges, preferably of different colors, are needed. One is for wiping around the eyes, the nose, and the muzzle—do not use this sponge on another horse, as this could result in the spread of respiratory infections. The other sponge is for wiping the dock area, around the tail.

Grooming Essentials

Body brush—short bristles, soft in the center, harder at the edge

Stable cloth—this is a bit like a drying cloth

Plastic curry comb—with rows of short, tough plastic teeth

Sponges—in different colors or sizes for different jobs

Rubber curry comb—with short, flexible teeth in circles

Tail bandage—similar to a crepe bandage; store it neatly rolled

Hoof pick—a hoof pick with a brush does two jobs in one

Dandy brush—this has long, comparatively hard bristles

Water brush—with long, soft water-retentive bristles

Metal curry comb—with rows of metal teeth

Grooming kit box *Body brush* *Stable rubber*

Plastic curry comb

Sponges

Metal curry comb

Water brush *Dandy brush* *Hoof pick* *Tail bandage* *Rubber curry comb*

EYE WIPING

This should be carried out using a clean sponge dipped in tepid water and wrung out to prevent water from running down the face. It prevents tear-staining, and will also clean this area of the face. Wipe away from the eye itself.

NOSE AND MUZZLE CLEANING

Carefully wiping these areas will remove any trace of food or hay deposited here. This is also vital in the case of any nasal infections, but always reserve a sponge for each horse to prevent a possible spread of infection.

DOCK HYGIENE

A separate sponge should be used for this area. Any soiling here is especially serious, because fecal deposits will attract flies to lay their eggs, with the resulting maggots producing toxins that enter the horse's blood stream.

After a horse has been washed down (see pp.88–89), a sweat scraper is useful in forcing water out from the coat. Use the rubber side over more sensitive or bony parts, with the metal edge being applied over the rest of the body. The coat can then be given a final polish with a stable cloth.

Hoof pick

A hoof pick is essential to keep the feet clean, and should be brightly colored, so if it is dropped accidentally, it can be retrieved easily on the bedding—its sharp end might otherwise cause injury. Hoof oil will also be required, with a small paintbrush to apply it. Each hoof should be painted with water and then oil, which not only makes it look more attractive, but also aids recovery in cases where the hoof may be brittle or damaged.

Picking out Hooves

This is an essential task, helping to keep your horse sound as well as minimizing the risk of any infection developing on the underside of the foot. As a result, it is very important to train your horse to allow you to pick up, inspect, and clean its hooves without difficulty.

The hooves should be checked regularly and cleaned out as required. If dried mud has accumulated in this area, it will need to be brushed out.

Picking out the hooves needs to be carried out carefully, to prevent accidental injury, so work downward from the heel to the toe.

The grooming process

A horse requires daily grooming, the extent of which is influenced by the way in which it is being kept and the work it is doing. Full grooming, known as strapping, can take as long as 45 minutes and is normally carried out after a period of exercise. In some large stables, automatic grooming machines are available. These can assist the process, but their noise may be upsetting to horses that are not used to them. If you use such a machine, it is vital to bandage the tail first, and a circuit breaker must always be incorporated into the electrical supply.

Preparation

Grooming is normally carried out with the horse tied up and any blanket either removed or folded back, depending on the weather and whether you are outside in the yard or

Precautions to Take

Take care not to upset your horse when you are grooming its hindquarters, being particularly wary if it raises a foot off the ground, as this could indicate that it is about to lash out. As always, standing behind your horse is not recommended, since you are more vulnerable to being kicked. Although young horses especially can sometimes prove rather excitable when being groomed, if you always follow a distinct routine, starting at the head and working backward, your horse will soon come to recognize that it has nothing to fear. Temperament can be significant, with heavy horses generally proving more amenable to being groomed than Arabs or Thoroughbreds, for example, thanks to their more placid natures.

Grooming

Start grooming your horse at the top of his neck, and work down. A muddy horse will need cleaning off with a dandy brush or curry comb to start with, and you can then tidy up with a body brush. Next, concentrate on the mane. First, brush it onto the wrong side of the neck and groom the underlying hair, before starting to comb the longer hair in strands. The tail will also need some attention, although regular brushing of the long hair is not recommended since it will cause damage. This should be enough for going out on a hack. For more special occasions, add a final polish with a stable cloth.

Most horses enjoy being groomed and will stand still or even doze while they are being brushed and cleaned up.

warm and dry in a stable. It is usual to start by picking out the hooves into a skep, adding this to the muck heap in due course. Hoof cleaning needs to be done twice daily, particularly when your horse is being brought into its stable from the field. If its lower limbs are very muddy, you may need to wash them—try not to use more water than necessary—and then dry them with an old towel. The basic grooming process is described below.

Finishing off

If you are not riding, once you have finished with the body brush, you may like to use a wisp or massage pad on your horse's muscles. Most horses really appreciate this attention and will be happy to doze for as long as you want to continue grooming. On most occasions, you should also wipe the eyes and nose with a damp sponge (see p.85). You also need to clean the dock and sheath on a regular basis.

Use a rubber curry comb to remove any dried mud from the horse's body. Start at the top of its head, between the ears, and work systematically down toward the extremities. Do not forget the legs, but be careful not to be rough or to tickle.

Now you can go over the horse with the body brush. Start on the neck, brushing the coat in short, circular strokes, and using a curry comb to clean the brush as you go. Stabled horses need only a quick brush with the body brush.

You can use a dandy brush instead of the curry comb, if your horse is not too dirty. Once you have removed or broken up the worst of the mud clumps with a curry comb, get the rest out with the dandy brush.

When you are happy that your horse is clean and neat, use a stable cloth to give the finishing touches and to make its coat shine. If you are planning to go to a show, you are now ready to start plaiting the mane and tail (see pp.90–91).

giving your horse
a bath

It is normally not recommended that you wash the horse's entire body, because this is likely to strip out the oils in the coat. In wet weather, these oils help to insulate the horse by draining rain off the hair, leaving a warm layer of air trapped close to the skin. In addition, they are responsible for the glossy sheen on the coat, which is associated with good health. On the rare occasions when a horse may have to be washed, it is important to dry it properly so it does not develop a chill.

Should a horse become saturated, by being trapped in a river, for example, its coat must be dried off thoroughly as soon as possible, and it is advisable to keep it covered up for at least a week afterward, to prevent it from becoming chilled. With ponies and horses that are kept outdoors throughout the year, it is important to be careful during grooming not to remove too much grease from the coat. For this reason, the body brush should not be used to any great extent on the body; a dandy brush is preferable, since it only strips out sweat and mud.

Thanks to their pale coloration, gray horses can be more vulnerable than other horses to showing areas of dirt in their coats, and so they will benefit from more frequent and thorough grooming.

Dear Equine Casebook

I know that I'm not supposed to wash my horse, but he always lies in his dung at night, and, as he is a gray, the stable stains on his legs look very unsightly. During the day in summer he rolls in the field and then gets green grass stains on his legs. I know grays show the dirt more easily than other colors, but I sometimes feel embarrassed to go out hacking with such a scruffy horse.
Yours sincerely, Cathy Floyd

Most stains on your horse's coat should be removable through brushing, especially once the mud or dung has dried, but if you do need to carry out localized washing, minimize the area that is made wet. First wash the dirt off using some soapy lukewarm water, remove excess water with a sweat scraper, and then dry the area with a towel. Always be particularly careful washing around the face, and do not use soap or shampoo, since they will cause discomfort if they get into the eyes.

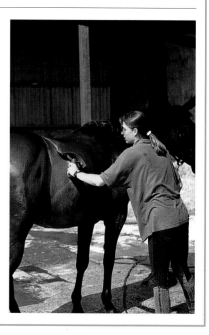

Dear Equine Casebook

My horse's tail is looking dreadful, with dried mud and other bits in it and lots of scurf and loose hair. I have heard that it is a good idea to wash the tail once in a while, but I am not sure how to go about it. Can you advise me?

Yours truly, Martin Cochrane

Washing the tail is generally a fairly straightforward procedure, especially if your horse is cooperative. It is simply a matter of partially filling a plastic bucket with lukewarm water and immersing the tail in it, before working in a mild shampoo. Use a water brush or sponge to wet the top of the tail area. Rinse the shampoo out thoroughly, shake out as much water as possible, and brush the tail along its length, using a body brush and concentrating on a few strands at a time. Finally, wrap it up in a tail bandage until it has dried.

Dear Equine Casebook

Recently, my very naughty pony got into a field that had had cows in it, and she managed to roll in some cow dung. After lots of brushing, I've managed to get it off most of her coat, but it is still stuck in her hair and along her neck, and it stinks! Please help.

Yours sincerely, Millie Fisher

The mane and surrouding area may need to be washed occasionally, and it sounds like this is one such time. Choose a day when the weather is warm and use a sponge and a mild shampoo, taking care that none of the water can run into your horse's eyes. A sweat scraper will be helpful to mop up water elsewhere as it runs out of the coat, after which the hair and neck should be dried with a towel.

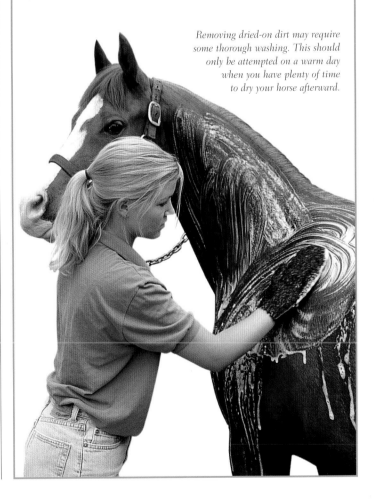

Removing dried-on dirt may require some thorough washing. This should only be attempted on a warm day when you have plenty of time to dry your horse afterward.

plaiting
manes and tails

A horse that is being shown or is taking part in competition should look its best, so it will need additional grooming, and except in the case of some pony breeds, this usually includes plaiting the mane and sometimes also the tail. Normally, the mane is allowed to lie naturally, but plaiting helps to highlight the crest and the outline of the neck, which makes the horse look neater and more attractive. For plaiting, you will need a blunt-ended needle and some thread that matches the color of your horse's mane. It is worth practicing mane pulling and plaiting before the day of the show, so both you can do neatly and quickly.

Pulling the mane

Before plaiting, the mane must be pulled. This must be carried out carefully over the course of several days, to prevent the area from becoming sore. Pulling is a process whereby the longer, more straggling, hairs are removed to produce a level mane that lies in a neat line along the neck. It has to be done by hand with the hairs not being cut at all. It is easier on a hot day or following exercise, when the pores are open, and it often helps to watch

PULLING A MANE

Before plaiting, you need to pull any long or straggling hairs from the mane. Push most of the hair up out of the way with a comb and remove the long strands a few at a time along the neck. Repeat until you have a neat, straight mane.

PLAITING THE MANE

Once you are ready to start plaiting, divide the hair into rough bunches. Thread your blunt-ended needle before beginning plaiting. Make three main strands from each clump and plait them together as you would any hair.

ROLLING THE PLAITS

When you reach the end of each plait, tie the thread around the tip and then fold the plait up and stitch it to itself, refold, and stitch again. Do this as many times as necessary to complete the plait so you have a neat topknot shape.

LEFT: A gypsy plait is a distinctive style whose origins can be traced back to the Romany community.

ABOVE: Certain plaits, such as this Arab plait, are linked to particular horse types, complementing their appearance.

someone carry out this task before attempting it yourself. It is important only to pull the long hair from the underside of the mane, rather than the top hairs; those left at the top will otherwise stand up, forming a ridge, and unsightly tufts will appear when the pulled ones regrow.

How to plait a mane

Once it has been thinned and shortened as necessary, the mane should be damped down with a brush, and then you can plan where the plaits will fall. Each bunch of hair should be about as wide as a mane comb, allowing for a forelock plait and an uneven number of plaits running down the neck itself (see left).

How to plait a tail

The tail may also occasionally need to be plaited, but it is not always advisable to pull it—many horses resent this. It is important to assess at the outset whether the tail can be plaited successfully—long hairs must be evident at the sides of the dock. Before you begin plaiting, brush the tail and dampen the hair as you would for plaiting a mane.

How to Plait a Tail

Although it looks quite complicated, tail-plaiting is fairly easy to do, as long as you take your time and make the plait as tight as possible. There are a number of variations on the theme (see below right), but the one shown here is probably the most popular and straightforward.

Divide part of the tail into three small bunches, one on either side and one top. Work in bunches of hair from each side of the tail, as you plait downward. After completing about three-quarters of the length of *the dock, stop taking in new hair and continue until what you have in your hands is finished. Once you reach the end, tie the plait with thread, loop it up, and tuck it behind itself. Then sew it in place.*

Putting Up

If there is a risk that the tail could become very muddy or get in the way during work—such as on the polo field or across country—a modified form of plaiting, called "putting up," is used. The plait is continued to the end of the tail and then rolled back up to the dock, where it is doubled up and held in place with stitches or tape, making sure it lies flat at the level of the tail vertebrae.

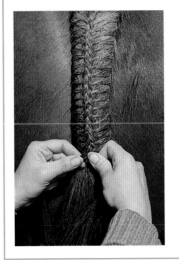

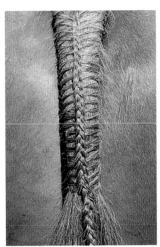

clipping
a winter coat

A horse's coat becomes significantly thicker for the winter. This means that vigorous exercise during this period can lead to excessive sweating and then chilling. Making the coat shorter through clipping avoids this problem, although the horse will then need to be warmly covered with a blanket, particularly if it is turned out. In the northern hemisphere, a first clip is usually carried out in October, with further clipping on roughly a monthly basis through to January. Clipping at a later stage will affect the spring coat.

Preparing to clip

The noise of the clippers and the unfamiliar sensations may upset a horse that has never been clipped before. If you are also inexperienced, ask someone who has clipped a

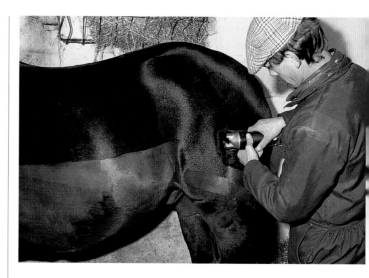

Clipping is a straightforward procedure, but it can be upsetting for nervous horses, so approach the task cautiously. Be sure the clippers are sharp before starting.

Types of Clip

There are a number of different types of clip. A full clip is when all the hair is removed from the body. A variation on this is the hunter clip, which leaves a saddle patch and longer hair on the legs, affording some protection against cuts when hunting. In the blanket, clip an area of long hair in the shape of a blanket on the body is left. Blanket clips offer more protection against the cold, although blankets will still be required. Trace clips in various styles leave the horse with shorter hair on the lower neck and body, and are often recommended for horses spending the winter out at grass.

A gullet clip extends from under the lower jaw to the belly. It is commonly used on ponies.

The hunter clip leaves longer hair on the legs, as well as a distinctive saddle patch.

The blanket clip creates a blanketlike layer of longer hair on the body, and sometimes on the head.

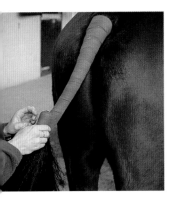

For tail bandaging, the bandage is wound around and down the tail.

The bandage is held in place by being tied in a knot as shown here.

horse to do the first clip, rather than attempting to do it yourself. In any case, do not attempt to clip on your own, but ask someone to assist by holding the horse. Wear old clothes and rubber-soled boots; a dust mask may also be advisable, particularly if you are sensitive to animal hair.

The clippers must be well-maintained, with the blades sharpened after each full clip. They will need oiling and possibly tightening as well, prior to use. The clip may take more than 45 minutes to complete, and the clippers can become very hot, so you will need to pause at intervals to apply a special coolant.

Clipping needs to be done where there is adequate space to move easily around the horse, and good light, but it should not be done outdoors. The floor must be level and not slippery, and electricity must be easily accessible. A circuit breaker is vital. It is much safer to have the cord threaded on hooks in the ceiling, to be pulled down as necessary, rather than dragging on the floor.

Starting a clip

Depending on the type of clip (see box, left), the process usually begins on the shoulders and goes against the direction of the hair. Always bandage the tail before starting out. Where the skin is not flat, clip with particular care—stretching the skin with your hand can help to prevent nicks. Potentially difficult areas, such as the groin, should

Rugs and Their Uses

There are many different types of rug available, most designed with a particular purpose in mind.

OUTDOOR BLANKETS
Outdoor blankets are usually made of ripstop, light, quick-drying materials, and can be made warmer by putting a liner underneath. They generally give good protection against the elements, but must fit well to prevent slipping. Exercise blankets (right) keep a horse dry or warm when it is being ridden.

STABLE BLANKETS
Stable blankets are used to keep stabled horses warm overnight. Those that are easily washable are usually best, although the traditional jute blankets tend to be more durable. Jute usually requires an underblanket. They are anchored with a roller, whereas modern synthetic blankets have surcingles.

OTHER BLANKETS
Stabled horses may also wear day blankets during the day and for traveling. These are usually made of wool and buckled at the front, with a roller over the back. After vigorous exercise, a sweat or cooler blanket (right) can be used to help any sweat evaporate quickly, while still keeping the horse warm.

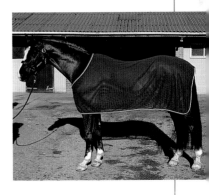

be left until last, to minimize any upset to the horse. Never clip inside the ears. Slightly overlap each stroke to make sure you do not miss any hair. Use a blanket to keep the horse warm as you proceed, and when you are finished, go over its body with a stable cloth to remove any loose hair.

feeding hay
and other bulk foods

To meet their nutritional needs, horses naturally spend relatively long periods eating each day. Their grazing habits are influenced by the seasons. During the summer, they eat during the day, tending to rest at night. The converse is true in the winter: they will graze at night, which is when the weather is coldest, their movements helping to keep them warm. They then rest during the relative warmth of the day. It is not, therefore, a cause for concern that your horse appears to be grazing less when you see it during the hours of daylight in the winter months.

Hay and haylage

Horses require bulk and roughage in their diet, and if this cannot come from grazing grass, it must be supplied in the form of hay or haylage. Good-quality meadow hay, comprising a variety of grasses, including rye grass and other components, such as clover, is often used. Care should be taken that it does not contain poisonous plants. This is unlikely to be the case with seed hay, which is grown specially for making hay, rather than being cut from an established paddock (see box, right). Other types of hay such as alfalfa can be of higher nutritional value, and you will probably need to adjust the amount of concentrates in the horse's diet as a consequence. Another richer food is haylage, which needs to be introduced in small quantities.

Horses feed naturally by grazing, consuming both grass and herbage.

Dear Equine Casebook

Recently, my horse has been diagnosed as suffering from COPD. He's been treated by the vet, and I've been told that he will never fully recover. I understand that dust from hay will make the condition worse and wonder if you can give me any ideas on feeding to avoid this?
Sincerely, Penny Aldridge

When a horse is suffering from COPD, it can help to soak his hay for about 12 hours before feeding it to him. This is most easily accomplished by putting a full haynet in a container of clean water. Let it drain afterward; otherwise, it will be very heavy to lift. If you can find a good supplier, you might consider feeding haylage.

Another alternative is to buy semi-wilted grass, which is vacuum-packed and free from dust. Once the pack is opened, it must be used rapidly before the contents deteriorate; damaged packs should never be fed to horses. This type of grass contains more protein than hay, so it can be fed in smaller quantities.

Hay must always be stored in a dry place, such as a barn. The disadvantage of this barn is that it will be very dusty.

Hay

Seed hay or meadow hay are common choices for feeding horses. If you choose to feed meadow hay, be sure it comes from a reliable source so you do not need to worry about it containing poisonous plants, particularly the very dangerous ragwort (see p.109).

Seed hay (far right) is paler than meadow hay (right) and has a higher nutritional value. Beware of hay that looks brownish or very dark yellow, as this indicates that it is old and its nutritional value will have declined.

Although it is generally recommended that hay is fed on the floor because this is a more natural way for a grazing animal to eat, hay nets are still popular since they keep the hay in one place and make the horse eat more slowly. They must be tied up carefully.

Quality

It pays to be fussy over the quality of your hay. Old hay, for example, not only has relatively little nutritional value, but will also be heavily contaminated by dust and mold spores. These are likely to be harmful to your horse, being the cause of the condition known as chronic obstructive pulmonary disease (COPD) or heaves—this latter name due to the way in which the horse's breathing becomes labored. The damage to the lungs is irreversible, and the horse will appear worse at different times, especially during hot weather. COPD also usually causes a long-standing cough, and often a discharge from the nostrils. Although it is difficult to assess the quality of hay, unless it is obviously very dusty, it should have a sweet smell and appear light greenish-brown; old hay is a decidedly yellowish or brown shade.

Aging hay

Hay must not be fed as soon as it is made because it will be difficult to digest. It needs to be at least six months old, and preferably nearer to a year, to reduce the risk of colic. As a further precaution to protect the horse's health, mix old hay with the new, when your stocks are running out. Haylage must also be allowed to age for about six to eight weeks before being given.

giving your horse
concentrated foods

When a horse is working hard, it is unable to meet all of its nutritional requirements solely from hay and grass, which is why its diet needs to be supplemented with concentrates. These provide additional energy and protein, as well as vitamins and minerals.

Formulated feeds

There are many different types of cubes (or nuts) and coarse mixes, each with carefully formulated ingredients to meet the nutritional needs of horses undertaking a variety of tasks. They are commercial preparations, generally available from equestrian outlets and agricultural merchants. They are quick and easy to feed, not requiring any preparation, so many people choose to use these mixes, rather than the individual grains or cereals. However, it is vital to match the type of feed to your horse's requirements. These are usually described on the packaging, but if you have any doubts, ask the retailer for advice before buying. It is important to check the expiration date for the

vitamins; this will be stamped on the packaging. Do not be tempted to buy a large sack that will go out of date before its contents can be consumed by your horse—coarse mixes tend to deteriorate more rapidly than cubes. Store feed sacks in a dry place out of the reach of rodents. Metal trash cans are useful for this.

How much to feed

Cubes or coarse mixes can constitute your horse's or pony's entire concentrate ration. A little water should be used to dampen the food—too much will make cubes break up. The quantity to feed is given on the packaging, and should not be exceeded. It is advisable to add some chaff (well chopped hay or straw) to cubes or coarse mixes to prevent them from being eaten too fast. If your horse persists in trying to eat rapidly, try placing a brick in its food bowl. The effort of eating around the brick will slow it down.

Traditional feeds

Oats, barley, chaff, bran, linseed, and sugarbeet are traditional horse feeds, and they are normally given as a mixture to provide a balanced diet (see pp.97–99 for detailed preparation instructions).

The level of concentrates in the diet will be influenced by the amount of work the horse undertakes.

Types of Feed

There are a number of different foodstuffs that are used as concentrates for horses. These include oats, barley, bran, alfalfa, linseed, and sugarbeet. However, it is important to remember that, unlike cubes and similar foods, these are not supplemented with additional vitamins and minerals, and therefore cannot be considered as balanced foods. They may need to be mixed before use.

Alfalfa chaff is prepared by using a chaff cutter, which cuts the stems into suitably small pieces. You can mix the alfalfa chaff with molasses.

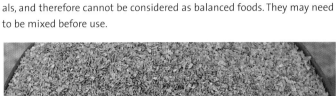

Bran provides bulk in a horse's diet and can help to correct loose droppings if fed in a dry state. More commonly, however, it is fed as a wet mash.

Be sure to match the formulated nuts and coarse mix to your horse's needs, and feed according to the instructions.

Rolled barley increases the choice of feeding options. It is also sometimes used in a crushed form as an alternative to oats.

Rolled oats are the most widely used of the grains fed to horses, with rolling helping to increase their digestibility.

Dried sugarbeet pulp is sold in the form of cubes, which must be soaked before use. Buy in small quantities since they become moldy fairly quickly.

It is important that horse food is kept dry and in clean surroundings to deter rodents. Use the bags in strict rotation so the food content does not deteriorate.

Oats

Oats need to be given in moderation, particularly to ponies, because they can cause excitability, making the animal more lively than usual. Whole oats cannot be digested easily, so they are usually fed crushed or rolled. Their nutritional value declines in this state, however, so do not stock up with more than three weeks' supply at a time.

Dear Equine Casebook

I have been feeding my horse with a good-quality coarse mix to which I add some chaff and, occasionally, sugarbeet. Although he seems generally very healthy, his grazing is restricted, and I want to be sure that he is getting all the vitamins and other nutrients that he needs.
Yours sincerely, Alan Johnstone

If you are using any one of the many good-quality formulated mixes, there is little need to worry over vitamin and mineral intake, although it is still a good idea to provide a salt lick, which your horse will rasp with its tongue, and gnaw. In fact, it is not usually recommended to provide any other vitamin and mineral supplement, for fear of overdosing, which can be potentially harmful in the long term.

Barley

Barley, which is prepared in a similar way to oats, provides another feeding option. It should never be given whole unless it has been boiled. Flaked barley is popular, and it can be used as a substitute for some of the oats in a ration, being less likely to trigger hyperexcitability.

Chaff and bran

If your horse rushes its food without chewing it properly before swallowing, then consider adding some chaff. Bran, too, can be beneficial in slowing down a fast eater. It should not be fed in large quantities on a regular basis though, because it interferes with calcium absorption from the intestines. If offered dry, bran can help to firm up the droppings if necessary; as a mash, it can act as a laxative. A mash is made with about 2lb (1kg) of bran, adding enough boiling water to give it a moist consistency. Stir the mixture well and leave it to cool before feeding. If your horse is not used to eating bran, the addition of some linseed jelly should make it more palatable.

This type of food bowl greatly simplifies the task of feeding a large number of stabled horses. Each bowl can be filled without having to enter the stable.

Linseed

Linseed itself is especially favored for creating a healthy gloss on the coat, although it is poisonous until cooked. The jelly is made by soaking the linseed in water for 24 hours before bringing it to a boil and simmering it for several hours. It is allowed to cool and then added to the evening feed. One pound (0.5kg), covered with about 4in (10cm) of water, will produce enough for one feed. It all needs to be used within 24 hours. Sometimes, linseed is prepared alongside boiled barley.

Sugarbeet

Sugarbeet pulp also needs to be prepared carefully. It must be very well soaked, because otherwise it can cause choking or may swell up in the horse's digestive system. Use cold water for soaking, adding no more than 1lb (0.5kg) of sugarbeet pulp to half a bucket of water, and leave it to stand for 12 hours. The soaked sugarbeet must be fed immediately, because it starts to ferment—a process speeded up by hot water. If you buy sugarbeet cubes, they need to be soaked until they have disintegrated.

Carrots and other fresh foods

Although horses should ideally be allowed to graze daily, this is not always possible. Especially during the winter months, you may need to supplement their diet with other fresh foods, such as carrots. They should be cleaned before being sliced lengthwise. Never make small, circular pieces, as these may cause choking. The same applies with apples.

Fact File

FEEDING REGIMEN

While hay can be almost constantly available, the daily concentrate ration is normally divided into three feeds, which are offered at regular times throughout the day. Stabled horses should not be fed just prior to exercise, so the day should start with a relatively small feed, and a restricted quantity of hay. Exercise can safely begin about 90 minutes later. A larger meal should be given afterward, with the hay net being filled, and then a third meal toward the end of the afternoon.

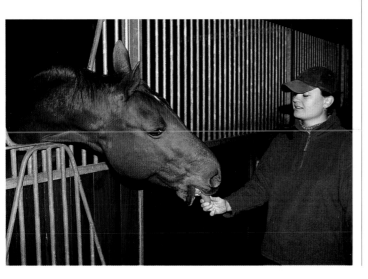

Horses will enjoy the attention of being fed tidbits, but be sure this type of food is safely prepared first and beware that you do not get bitten. This can happen quite easily, especially if the horse is impatient for its treat.

stabling
and the stable yard

Although it is sometimes possible to use a shed or other outbuilding for stabling your horse, some conversion work may be necessary first. For example, insulation may need to be added to brick buildings, not just in the roof but to the walls as well. This will keep the temperature more even in hot summers and cold winters. Above all, drafts must be excluded. Even so, ventilation is very important to the horse's wellbeing, to minimize the risk of respiratory infections, and the interior needs to have good natural lighting.

The ideal stable

For a horse, the ideal stable needs to have a floor area of at least 12 x 14ft (3.5 x 4.5m). Any smaller, and the horse may not be able to stand up again if it slips over for any reason.

The ceiling needs to be approximately 10ft (3m) above ground level. The stable door opening should be a minimum of 4ft (1.5m) wide and about 8ft (2.5m) high. This will allow the horse to go through it easily without risk of injury.

Traditional stable doors are hinged in two parts: the upper section opens on its own to provide ventilation, while the lower section is normally kept closed when the stable is occupied. The lower section should be high enough that a horse or pony cannot climb out, but low enough that the same animal can see over it and watch what is going on in the vicinity, which will help prevent boredom. For security, there should be a bolt on the upper door; the lower door should have both a bolt at the top and a kick bolt that can be operated easily with a boot close to

ABOVE: *A typical row of stables, with good access at the front to allow the horses to be led in and out easily. They afford plenty of ventilation.*

LEFT: *High-tech, purpose-built American barn stabling. Note the wide access doors and external covered areas.*

the bottom (see box on p.102). All the bolts and hinges in a stable must be kept well-oiled to prevent them from sticking or rusting.

Ventilation

Additional ventilation can be provided by windows, which are best built facing south to avoid cold winds. As a further precaution against drafts, they need to be relatively high and should be louvered to open inward. On the inside, the window needs to be protected by bars, particularly if it is glass. This will prevent the horse from breaking the glass, which should in any case be reinforced with mesh.

Neatness and Safety

Neatness in the stable yard is very important, not just for the sake of appearances, but also for the horse's safety as well as your own. The yard should be swept regularly, and any tools stored away after they have been used. Pitchforks especially can be very dangerous if left lying around because of their sharp prongs. The same applies to hoses, which can cause both people and horses to stumble. In cold weather, it is very important to make sure the hard surface outside the stables remains free of ice. Otherwise, it can become an additional hazard.

Bolts and Hinges

The perfect stable is equipped with a variety of bolts to keep the horse safely inside when required. They must also be easy to open in the case of an emergency. For example, with practice, it is quicker to kick open the lower bolt than bend down and slip it open. Cabin hooks should also be put in to make sure the doors stay safely open when required.

A kick bolt at the bottom of the door provides added security against the horse learning to open the door, or kicking it open or catching its hoof.

Draw bolts on both the upper and lower door of a stable. The eyes above and below are for cabin hooks, another vital piece of stable furniture.

Roofing

The interior of the stable needs to be dry, whatever the weather, so the roof should be sloped and should overhang slightly at the front of the stable. Guttering should be put in to take rainwater away. This also makes it easier to attend to the horse's needs when it is raining hard.

Fixtures

Inside the stable a tie-ring needs to be put on the wall approximately 5ft (1.5m) off the floor. Never tie your horse to a tie-ring. Instead tie a piece of string to the tie-ring and fasten your horse's lead rope to this. The string serves as a safety device. If your horse spooks in its stable when tied up, it will break to prevent the horse from being injured by its head collar. When not needed for tying up, the ring can be used for the hay net, which needs to be put at the horse's eye level. It should not be any higher; otherwise,

Well-ventilated and light internal stables where the horses can see what is going on around them.

The Ideal Stable

- The floor surface must be durable and textured so that it is not slippery.
- Include a very gentle slope to allow for drainage.
- Gullies need to run outside, and must be kept clear of bedding.
- Options other than concrete may be worth considering.
- Do not site a drain under the hay net as it will become easily blocked.

small pieces of hay may fall into the horse's eyes. Some people prefer to feed hay on the floor in any case. Feed concentrates in a corner manger or in a tub on the floor. Water must be provided in a separate bucket, which should have a capacity of at least 2 gallons (9 liters).

Stalls

Although many horses are kept in individual stables, in some establishments they may be housed in stalls in a larger building. Stalls, as their name suggests, are partitioned areas, and horses are kept in them with a head collar and lead rope. To prevent the lead rope from becoming entangled, it is threaded through the tie-ring, and a weight

Safe Electrical Supply

Having an electrical supply to stables is vital on winter evenings and for carrying out clipping and similar tasks. Safety is a very important consideration from the outset. Any electrical work should be undertaken by a professional electrician who will install equipment designed for use outside, such as waterproof switches and sockets. If you do not wish to go to the expense of installing an electrical supply, reliable battery-operated lights are obtainable. The stable lights should be located right up in the roof, where they will give off a good light with little shadow. A switch should be positioned outside the stable door, out of the horse's reach, so you can turn the light on before entering the area.

is attached to the loose end. As the horse approaches the ring, the weight falls toward the ground, taking the slack with it so there is no loose rope. Most stalls also have a conventional tie-ring approximately 5ft (1.5m) high.

Ventilation can be a problem when it comes to housing a number of horses in a single unit. It is made worse by the fact that such an environment inevitably has a larger accumulation of muck and associated ammonia levels. Ammonia can damage the horse's respiratory tract, making it more susceptible to infection, and where ventilation is poor, infections will spread more rapidly through a group. A horse in its own stable is likely to enjoy better ventilation and also be less vulnerable to contagious infections.

Horses housed in stalls rather than stables are more likely to become bored. Entry to the stall is from a central passageway.

bedding
– which sort is best?

There are four main types of bedding available for covering the stable floor: straw, shavings, paper, and rubber matting. A number of other variations include hemp and flax.

Straw

Thanks to its low cost, straw is still very commonly used for bedding, in spite of newer options. There are three types of straw: wheat, barley, and oat. Wheat straw is often favored, partly because it is less likely to be eaten by the horse. It is also relatively tough, so it drains well, rather than becoming saturated when wet, which tends to be the

LEFT: You will need to remove all the droppings in the stable and also the wet bedding each day.

RIGHT: Shavings are an alternative to straw, but watch out for any odd sharp pieces of wood.

Mucking-out Tools

A variety of tools will be useful for mucking-out, and they are widely available from saddle shops and similar outlets. Shovels are needed for clearing up droppings, while forks are essential for moving straw and organizing the muck heap. A sturdy brush is required for sweeping up.

Shovel   Short fork   Yard brush

Long folk   Pitchfork   Pitchfork   Shavings fork

case with both oat and barley straw. Both these latter types also often contain prickly bristles that can result in skin irritation in humans and horses.

Straw bedding is easy to manage. Take out the droppings and soiled straw each day, adding extra bedding as necessary. The stable should be cleaned out completely each week. When you add new bedding, always break up the bales thoroughly. If your horse starts to eat the straw, try placing old straw on top of the new as a deterrent.

Shavings and paper

If your horse suffers from respiratory problems, shavings or paper are a better choice than straw, since they are relatively free from dust. Shavings are supplied in large plastic-wrapped bales, which can be stored in a dry place until required. Paper bedding in various forms has become more popular over recent years. Although based on recycled products, it is still relatively expensive. It has good

Clean the stable thoroughly every week, removing all the bedding, and washing and disinfecting the floor. A sturdy, good-sized wheelbarrow will simplify this task.

Muck Heap

Management of the muck heap is important, especially in a large yard, where the volume of material to be disposed of will be significant. The heap itself should be located some distance from the stables because it will tend to smell, especially in warmer weather, and looks unsightly. Over a period of time, the bedding will rot down, providing valuable garden manure. It helps if the muck heap can be divided into sections so that each can be filled in turn, rather than simply adding to one existing pile, which means manure can be removed more easily.

absorbency, but this can be a drawback when mucking out, because it is very heavy when damp. Another disadvantage is that some inks could cause an allergic skin reaction.

As with straw, shavings or paper bedding must be spot-cleaned daily, and the surface raked to prevent it from becoming compacted. Drains can get blocked by paper and may need to be covered when cleaning out the stable.

Rubber matting
One of the most hygienic forms of bedding available is rubber matting. This was originally devised for use in horse trailers, but is now available for putting over the floor of a stables. It is reasonably warm and can be supplemented as necessary with just a thin layer of more conventional bedding, such as straw, on top, lessening the problem of

waste disposal. If by itself, it can be hosed down very easily, and also provides a surface on which horses are unlikely to slip.

Deep littering
Rather than a weekly clearout, some horse owners operate what is known as a deep-litter system. This not only saves time, but also uses less bedding material. However, it is vital that the droppings are removed daily and fresh bedding added. It is also important to keep a close check on the horse's feet, to make sure infections do not develop.

keeping your horse
at grass

To have plenty of space and food, each horse needs 1.5–2 acres (0.6–0.8 hectares) of grass. It is not a good idea to keep a horse in a field alone, because it is unlikely to settle well in isolation, so you will need to multiply these figures by the number of horses you will be keeping to arrive at the amount of land required.

Fencing

The perimeter of the field must be securely fenced. A hedge with a post-and-rail fence makes the best boundary, with the hedge providing protection from the worst of the elements. Where this combination is not possible, a post-and-rail fence, three rails high, is recommended. Provided that it is at least 4ft (1.5m) high, most horses will not attempt to jump out.

Wire can be used instead of wooden rails, but never barbed wire, which can be very dangerous if the horses panic in the field and get caught up on it. The sharp projections are also likely to tear blankets if the horse brushes against them. Broad-mesh sheep fencing is also potentially dangerous if a horse puts one of its feet through the mesh. To guarantee a long life and security, all lumber should be treated with a non-toxic wood preservative, and the posts must be set 2ft (0.6m) into the ground. Rotting wood or shallowly set posts can fall down, allowing the horses to escape from the field.

Gates

Entry to the paddock should be through a gate of the same height as the fence and at least 10ft (3m) wide. If possible, the gate should be sited on well-drained or high ground, because the horses will often congregate around it, awaiting their meals, so if it is in a low, damp corner, it will soon become a morass of mud in wet weather.

Be sure that gates are kept securely closed at all times.

Fencing and Boundaries

A number of different types of fencing may be employed around a field, sometimes combined with a natural hedge, giving horses somewhere to shelter when the weather is bad. Hedges offer more protection against the elements than a fence alone, though it can take years to become established, and a young hedge will present no effective barrier to a horse. It is also important to check that there are no poisonous plants in the hedge. Fencing needs to be well maintained to make sure that it, too, is both sturdy and safe for horses.

Field gates must be easy to open and close, as well as being wide enough to give easy access. Keep hardware well-maintained, with regular oiling of hinges.

Post-and-rail fences are traditionally made of wood and are a relatively expensive way of enclosing a field. A similar but rot-free plastic alternative is available.

The presence of trees, here behind post-and-rail fencing, offers good protection against the elements, especially when this barrier is north-facing. Look for windbreaks of this type when choosing a field for horses.

A horse alone in a field is less likely to become bored and look for ways out, if it is provided with toys that it can use to amuse itself.

Water

Since horses may drink about 9.5 gallons (36 liters) each day, providing water in the field is very important. If there is no piped supply available, you will have to bring it in each day, which is a laborious task. In this case, it helps if the water trough is located close to the fence, where you can fill it up more easily. It may be worthwhile considering having a pipe put in, with the location influenced by the cost of extending from the nearest source.

A field shelter

A field shelter may also be needed, particularly for horses that are living outside throughout the year. Not only does this provide them with somwhere to escape the worst of the elements, but also means their food can remain dry when the weather is wet. It will need to be slightly larger than a stable (see pp.100–103) and should have a solid floor of concrete or well-compacted earth. Two doors or one large entrance may be preferable, so that no single horse can monopolize the shelter.

maintaining a **healthy paddock**

Always make sure there is plenty of space, and grass, for each horse in the paddock (see p.106). Never be tempted to overcrowd a field, since this will leave the horses more exposed to the risk of parasitic infestations—especially worms, which can cause colic—as well as a loss of condition. The first animals to suffer are foals, and their growth may be permanently stunted as a result. The other effect of having too many horses in an enclosure is that the overgrazed grass will quickly get into a poor state. In

ABOVE: *The grass in this paddock represents good grazing for horses, but do not overlook parasite control, which is important in terms of their health.*

RIGHT: *A rather overgrazed meadow, which needs time to recover. An adequate area for grazing is vital to prevent one field from being completely stripped of grass.*

Poisonous Plants

Before turning the horses out in a paddock that has been rested, it pays to check it over for harmful plants. Cut back branches of yew, laburnum, and any other poisonous trees. Privet hedges can be equally dangerous. Although oak trees are not a problem themselves, horses can become ill from eating the acorns as they fall off the tree in late summer. You should, therefore, be prepared to rake them up regularly if there is a mature oak tree in your paddock.

RAGWORT AND OTHER PROBLEMS

One of the most common hazards in poorly maintained, overgrazed paddocks is ragwort, which has distinctive yellow flowers. Paddocks should be inspected in the spring for signs of young plants, which will need to be dug out, to prevent horses from eating them and suffering liver damage. Other plants that are potentially dangerous include deadly nightshade, which sometimes grows in hedges, and bracken. It pays to learn to recognize which poisonous plants grow in your area, so you can identify them.

PHOTOSENSITIVITY

Even plants that are not directly poisonous can cause problems, such as photosensitivity. St John's wort (*Hypericum*) is one of the best-known examples in this category. It contains a chemical that makes the skin react badly to sunlight, particularly relatively unpigmented areas of the coat. These areas then become badly inflamed and may slough off. Treatment involves keeping the horse in its stable, out of sunlight for a period, and removing the plants that are causing the problem.

Ragwort

Yew

Privet

Some common poisonous plants

- **Yew** Trees can easily overhang fields or may be growing in hedges.
- **Laburnum** Yellow bracts of flowers and long seed pods characterize this ornamental but deadly tree.
- **Ragwort** A common weed, with yellow flowers in late summer. Invades paddocks and must be dug out.
- **Deadly nightshade** This plant with tomatolike flowers followed by berries is often found in shade.
- **Bracken** This will be eaten by horses, especially if other greenery is in short supply. Can be in hay as well.
- **St. John's wort** Small yellow flowers characterize this plant, which can be found in meadows.
- **Privet** Tough, hardy green or variegated shrub used for hedging. May be present around fields.
- **Ivy** Grows widely in shade, normally as a climber.

addition, if the horses have insufficient food, they may resort to eating other plants in the vicinity, some of which may be poisonous (see box above).

Grass management

Along with a regular deworming schedule, frequent clearing-up of the horses's droppings in the field minimizes the risk of parasites becoming established. In some cases, resting and fertilizing the paddock may be enough to restore the condition of the grass. Harrowing can be beneficial, but be careful with weedkillers, which may have harmful effects, particularly if not used in accordance with the directions. If you need to reseed a paddock, be sure to choose a suitable mix for horses. It should include perennial rye grass.

a year in the life of
a field

The way in which horses and ponies at grass need to be looked after will vary through the year and may also differ from year to year, depending on the weather conditions.

Spring

In the early spring, hay and concentrates still need to figure prominently in the diet. When the grass starts to grow well, the level of concentrates can be reduced and hay can cease to be fed. At this time, great care needs to be taken with ponies, particularly those that have been kept inside over the winter. They are liable to succumb to laminitis (see p.40) through gorging themselves on new grass. Laminitis is more likely if they are allowed to become overweight, so it is a good idea to limit their access to grass, perhaps by keeping them in a paddock where there is less grazing available.

Summer

In the summer, the grazing is likely to be at its best, and as the temperature rises, so the horses will be drinking more.

The water trough will need to be emptied and refilled regularly, before the water turns green because of algal growth—especially as some forms of algae are toxic.

The warm weather also brings out flies. They can be particularly irritating to horses, congregating around the head and tail, which they flick repeatedly to deter the flies from settling. Flies do, however, have the benefit of encouraging a horse to keep moving, so it will take more exercise. Even so, offer some relief by using a suitable insect repellent.

As summer progresses, the grass will die back if the weather is very hot and dry, making good grazing harder for the horses to find. This is when they are at the greatest risk of eating toxic plants, which they would otherwise ignore. If there is little grass left in your fields, you may need to consider supplementing the

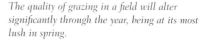

The quality of grazing in a field will alter significantly through the year, being at its most lush in spring.

horses' diet with hay or other forage. You need to take particular care in areas where the soil is sandy, because if the horse ingests any sand while browsing on very sparse grass, it can cause intestinal irritation, manifested as colic.

Fall and winter

There may be a lesser secondary flush of grass in the fall, and horses will often seek ripening fruit, such as blackberries, in hedges, undeterred by the thorns. Once winter descends, horses living outdoors will need to be covered up, as appropriate, against the cold. Increasing quantities of hay must be added to the diet to maintain condition, along with concentrates.

Offer the hay in well-spaced piles on the ground, rather than relying on a hay net in a field shelter. This allows all the horses to feed with minimal risk of disagreements. When it snows, horses will have great difficulty grazing and will be almost totally dependent on hay and concentrates.

ABOVE: During the winter, the field may be very muddy, and grazing will be difficult, especially during periods when there is snow on the ground.

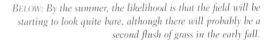

BELOW: By the summer, the likelihood is that the field will be starting to look quite bare, although there will probably be a second flush of grass in the early fall.

basic first aid
for horses

Horses often acquire minor cuts, either as the result of injuries out working or in their home environment. These will usually stop bleeding quite readily, particularly if you can apply pressure to the site of the injury, either with your hand or a clean handkerchief. Bear in mind that if your horse suffered a fall immediately before an injury, it is likely to be rather distressed, and you will probably need to concentrate on calming it down before dealing with the wound.

Tears of any kind are frequently the result of the horse being frightened and subsequently injuring itself on a sharp object. In a paddock, repeated minor injuries of this kind may be associated with bullying. Should the wound appear deep, however, it could have been caused by a projection such as a loose fence nail; cuts from glass or

cans usually have cleaner edges. If either of these injury types have occurred in a paddock, it is important to try to find the cause, so they will not happen again.

Minor wounds

Where the horse's tetanus vaccination is up to date and the wound is not huge, you may be able to treat it yourself and then leave it

A horse's incisor teeth are sharp, and a bite from them can easily puncture the skin, causing injury.

Basic Equipment

Essentials for the stable yard are antiseptic and wound powders for less serious injuries. A selection of dressings is also recommended, particularly to keep flies off minor wounds, plus a round-ended pair of scissors to cut dressings. A thermometer is useful. Prepare a portable first-aid kit for traveling.

CLEANING A WOUND

It is important to clean a wound thoroughly to minimize the risk of infection, especially on the lower limbs, where it can easily become contaminated with mud. Careful cleaning also allows you to check the extent of the wound to assess any other injury and make sure no splinter or other foriegn body is lodged in the area. Anything like this will have to be removed.

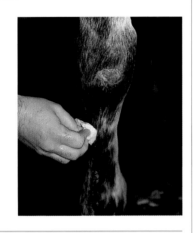

STITCHING

Your vet will stitch the wound in just the same way as if you had a bad cut. Stitching helps to draw the ends of skin together, facilitating the healing process, and also reduces the likelihood of contamination of the wound. The stitches can be removed painlessly after about seven to ten days, once the wound has healed well.

WIRE SCARRING

Although stitching a small area usually results in no very obvious scar, the risk of permanent disfiguration is likely where the injury is much more extensive, as here, where the wound was caused by this horse having been caught up around its neck in barbed wire. Barbed wire should never be used to fence a field containing horses, because it is so dangerous.

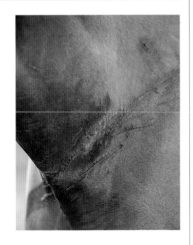

to heal by itself. To assist the healing process, clean the area thoroughly. Use blunt-tipped scissors to cut back the surrounding hair so it does not become incorporated into the scab. Bathe the wound as necessary, applying an antiseptic ointment afterward. During the summer, wounds often attract flies, so it is advisable to use a cream that incorporates an insecticide to prevent maggots from attacking the area. If you suspect that the wound is becoming septic, seek veterinary advice, as further treatment, including antibiotics, may be necessary.

Major wounds

More extensive wounds will need not just cleaning, but also suturing. While minor wounds will heal without a blemish, those that have to be stitched are more likely to show residual scarring. Urgent veterinary is needed in cases where blood is pumping out in large volumes, as this indicates that an artery has been severed. In this instance, while waiting for the vet to arrive, you should bind up the wound and apply pressure to restrict blood loss and, therefore, increase the horse's chances of survival. Try to calm your horse as much as possible, which should also help to prevent blood loss.

Joint injuries

On occasions, a horse can be unlucky enough to sustain an injury that penetrates into a joint, rather than being confined to the muscle tissue. Joint injuries are potentially very serious. A heavy fall while jumping a hedge out hunting, for example, may cause a fracture as well as bleeding. If your horse has obvious difficulty in walking after a fall or other accident, veterinary advice will need to be sought. However, the most important thing initially is to catch the horse and try to calm it down, to minimize any risk of worsening its injuries.

lameness
and the foot

Horses suffer from lameness for a variety of reasons. When you are riding, you will notice almost immediately if your horse becomes lame, because its foot fall will be uneven. However, it may not immediately be obvious which leg is affected. This can be determined by having someone walk your horse up and down, allowing you to view it from the side. If the lameness is in the front, when the affected leg makes contact with the ground, the horse will try to lessen the pain by lifting its head up, putting it down when the

Diagnosis

You need to be able to pick up your horse's feet easily to examine them in a case of lameness. It may be an acute condition, which comes on suddenly, suggesting an injury to the underside of the foot, or it could be a long-standing condition, which flares up on occasions. Stones in the feet are a common cause of sudden lameness and can usually be removed easily.

Cleaning off the hoof may give a clearer indication of the cause; take care as the foot may be more sensitive than usual.

Start by checking the foot when a horse goes lame, as the cause may be obvious.

sound leg takes over. Where the lameness is in a hindleg, there is a similar scenario, with the hock and hip being kept higher off the ground than normal when the painful leg comes down, resulting in a shorter stride. Short stride is also a feature when both forelegs are affected by lameness, as the horse is reluctant to put more of its body weight on them than necessary.

Finding the cause

When faced with a horse that has suddenly gone lame in one leg, start by examining the foot. It may well be that a stone has lodged under the shoe, causing bruising of the sole. This is why it is so important to act as soon as any hint of lameness emerges, because action taken at this stage can prevent a much more serious injury and a longer layoff. Lameness caused by bruising is worse when the horse is on uneven ground, where there is more variable contact with the surface, and on wet ground.

Treading on a sharp object, such as broken glass, may cause deep cuts in the underside of the foot. In addition to lameness, cuts like this can also lead to serious infection, so veterinary advice must be sought rapidly.

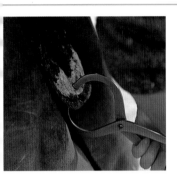

Hoof testers can be used to locate a painful spot on the foot, indicating that this is the affected area.

There is clear bruising of the sole in this case, which will need to be poulticed to assist its recovery.

If lameness emerges soon after shoeing, it is possible that a nail has damaged the sensitive laminae of the foot. Once the shoe is removed, the horse should soon become sound again, so do check with the blacksmith in this case.

Recurrent lameness

Some causes of lameness, such as corns, may become chronic, with regular recurrences. Corns can be related to poorly fitted shoes and inadequate hoof care, and their treatment may require special surgical shoes.

Laminitis is another typically recurrent reason for lameness, most commonly encountered in obese ponies. A diet based on meadow hay, rather than grass, is usually recommended in the case of an outbreak, which also causes distinctive rings to appear over the wall of the hoof.

Navicular disease is another chronic cause of lameness, arising from a poorly formed hoof, which damages the navicular bone at the back of junction between the pedal bone and short pastern (see p.35). Its rough surface then causes pain, affecting the flexor tendons, which is worse when the horse first starts working. There is relatively little that can be done for this arthritic problem.

Dear Equine Casebook

My horse went very lame recently. I called the vet who found that there was an abscess in the hoof. She cut a small hole in the hoof, and some pus came out. She then advised me to poultice the hoof for a couple of days until no more pus comes out. I have been poulticing, but have had trouble getting the bandages to stay on. Can you help?
Yours sincerely, Vincent Humphreys

It is easier to keep a poultice on if you stable your horse for the few days that the poultice is needed. Follow the simple steps below to make sure the bandage is firm and the dressing is in the right place. After you have stopped poulticing, it is a good idea to clean out the hole on a regular basis and, if possible, put a small piece of antiseptic-soaked cotton in it until it begins to heal up and grow over.

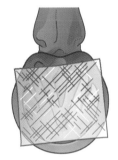

Step 1 Make sure the poultice is at the correct temperature by pressing it on to the back of your hand. If it is painfully hot, it needs to be allowed to cool before being applied on gauze, with a suitable dressing on top.

Step 2 You can then start to bandage the hoof, so the poultice remains in place, using a crepe bandage for this purpose. Applying petroleum jelly over the heel at the outset will help with the later removal of the poultice.

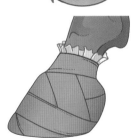

Step 3 The poultice is now secured in place with the bandage. If possible, fit a poultice boot to keep the bandage clean. Alternatively, you can use a stout plastic bag, with a pad at the front to stop it from being torn.

lameness
and the leg

The cause of lameness may be in the leg. This is where the advice of an experienced equine veterinarian can be invaluable in rapid identification of the source of the problem and advice on the best course of action, which is likely to involve rest. Initially, however, you can carry out an examination that may help to find the affected area.

Finding the source

Start by simply running your hands gently down the horse's limb, comparing it with the other one of the pair as necessary. Watch out for any indication of heat on the skin. This indicates underlying inflammation, and there could also be a growing swelling at the site. Be careful when examining the suspected site of lameness, because it may be painful, and your horse might lash out.

Many horses become lame as a result of strain injuries to the soft tissues of the limbs, such as the muscles, tendons, or ligaments. Reducing the risk of lameness is partly why it is essential to give them opportunity to warm up before undertaking exercise. Soft tissue injuries are most likely to occur when the horse is undertaking strenuous exercise, such as galloping or jumping.

Treatment

Never be tempted to work a horse with strain injuries. This sort of damage can take a year or even longer to repair. Seek advice from your vet, who will be well-placed to determine the

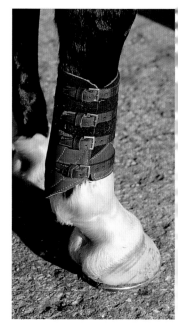

Brushing boots can be useful, especially when there is a conformational weakness where injuries can result from a foot brushing against one of the other legs.

Dear Equine Casebook

My vet has recently diagnosed my horse as having splints. Please can you tell me how he got them and whether they will affect his performance in the future? Also, can you tell me the difference between splints, spavins, and ringbone?
Yours truly, Laurence Smith-Parker

Splints are small, bony projections associated with the splint and cannon bones (see p.33). They often develop as the result of injuries, and although they initially result in lameness, it usually disappears once they have formed. Bone spavins, affecting the hock, and ringbones, on the pasterns, are similar. Bone spavins can lead to permanent lameness, inhibiting full flexion of the hock so the horse drags its foot. Ringbone is a bony swelling of the pastern and again reduces movement of this joint. A curb is associated with the hock joint, causing transient lameness and often linked with bad conformation. In this case, though, it is the ligament, rather than the bone, that becomes enlarged.

Stable Bandages

These bandages can be very beneficial, not just in terms of offering protection to the limbs, but also for improving the circulation. Stable bandages are usually put on all four legs, helping to warm them up. It is very important that they are applied correctly; otherwise, they can cause injury, especially to the tendons. Seek expert advice before using them for the first time if you are in any doubt. Padding must be wrapped around the leg first, before the bandage itself is applied on top.

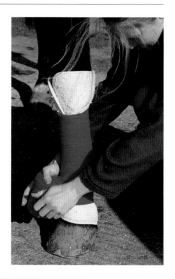

extent of the injury by using ultrasound equipment. Hosing the affected area with cold water can help to reduce the inflammation in the initial stages, with both legs of the pair wrapped in stable bandages.

Joint damage

Joint damage can also result in lameness, causing swelling of the sacs known as bursae, which contain the synovial fluid responsible for lubricating the joints themselves. Bursae are also found in association with tendons and vulnerable bony projections, such as the point of the hock in the hindlimb (see p.33), and they, too, can be subject to enlargement. If this occurs at the front of the hock, they are called bog spavins, while in the vicinity of the point of the hock, they are described as thoroughpins. On the fetlock, such swellings are referred to as windgalls. The horse needs to be rested. Cold hosing and massaging the affected area should resolve the problem.

Preventing Injury

There are a number of steps you can take to safeguard your horse from injury when you are out riding. There is a range of special equipment available for this purpose, but care needs to be taken that it is always fitted correctly. Knee-caps can be helpful, both for traveling and out on the road. The top strap has to be fitted to hold the boot in in place, while the lower strap is to make sure the boot cannot flap about. It must not be too tight because this would interfere with the joint movement.

Overreach boots safeguard the heels. They are made of rubber and extend around the lower pastern.

Knee caps, also known as knee boots, are traditionally made of leather and thick felt, to provide protection.

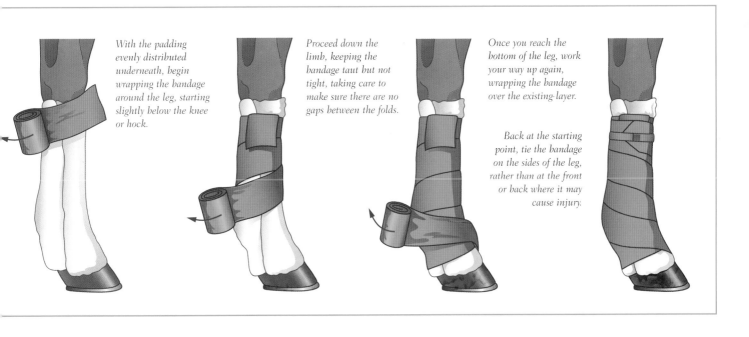

With the padding evenly distributed underneath, begin wrapping the bandage around the leg, starting slightly below the knee or hock.

Proceed down the limb, keeping the bandage taut but not tight, taking care to make sure there are no gaps between the folds.

Once you reach the bottom of the leg, work your way up again, wrapping the bandage over the existing layer.

Back at the starting point, tie the bandage on the sides of the leg, rather than at the front or back where it may cause injury.

recognizing
signs of illness

By spending time with your horse, you will become aware of its normal character and will notice very quickly if it becomes ill, because of changes in its appearance and behavior. Although much depends on the illness, there are a number of significant general signs. Any discharge from the eyes or nostrils, for example, should be treated suspiciously, particularly if coupled with coughing or other signs of respiratory distress. Excessive sweating and taut skin are

Problems with the Eyes and Nose

Discharges from the eyes or nose are always a cause for concern since they can indicate underlying disease. Although there may be a less worrying explanation, such as fly irritation, you should always be prepared to consult a vet when your horse has either of these symptoms.

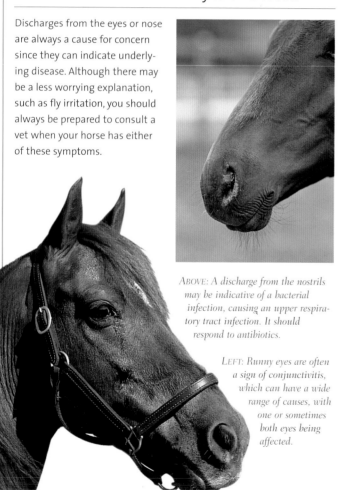

ABOVE: A discharge from the nostrils may be indicative of a bacterial infection, causing an upper respiratory tract infection. It should respond to antibiotics.

LEFT: Runny eyes are often a sign of conjunctivitis, which can have a wide range of causes, with one or sometimes both eyes being affected.

When you are familiar with your horse, you can quickly spot if it is not feeling well.

causes for concern, as are a loss of appetite and lack of thirst. A change in the color of the horse's urine, to a brown or reddish shade, for example, or alterations in the consistency of the droppings may require veterinary investigation. Difficulty in walking or any other signs of unusual behavior, such as pacing or attempting to kick at the underparts, must not be ignored.

An old horse is likely to be thinner and more bony, than a young one, so you need to be extra vigilant to see any signs of weight loss as they occur.

Taking a temperature

When you contact your vet, it can be helpful to relay information about the horse's temperature, which can be taken quite easily with an ordinary thermometer and a helper. Shake the thermometer down first, then dip it in a small quantity of petroleum jelly or a similar lubricant. Get your helper to hold the horse at the headcollar, before lifting its tail and sliding the bulb of the thermometer into its rectum so it lies against the rectum wall. Take care not to push it too far in; otherwise, it is likely to be pulled inside. Keep a firm grip on the thermometer throughout the minute that it is left in place. Remove it from the rectum, wipe it clean, and note the reading. A horse's normal temperature is approximately 100.5–101°F (38°C), and any increase of more than 1°F (0.5°C) indicates that it is raised.

Respiratory rate and pulse

When your horse is at rest, you can take its respiratory rate by measuring its chest movements over a minute. The figure should fall between 8 and 12 in total. Taking the pulse is slightly more difficult, and again the reading needs to be timed. It should work out at between 35 and 42 beats per minute in the resting horse. You may be able to locate the pulse from the artery running on the inside of

Indicators of Disease or Discomfort

If you suspect that your horse is off-color or ill, contact your vet. A horse's condition can deteriorate rapidly, which will extend the recovery period if it does not receive prompt attention.

Appetite—If your horse is grazing in a field, it can be difficult to check on how much it is eating. Should you suspect something is wrong, check the mouth first; there could be a dental problem.

Behavior—A horse that is in pain may start to behave strangely, and even aggressively if a sensitive part of its body is touched.

Bumps or swellings—It is important to determine the cause of a problem of this type, which could range from an insect bite to a tumor or injury.

Coat—Some parasites such as lice can localize here; the condition of the coat also provides insight into the horse's overall state of health.

Discharges—These are often linked with an infection and antibiotics may be required to overcome the bacteria responsible.

Dung and urine—The consistency of the dung and the color of the urine can both be indicators of the horse's state of health.

Eyes—Injuries to the eyes are not uncommon in horses, and they can even suffer from eyeworms (*thelaziasis*) on occasions.

Pulse—This provides an indication of the horse's overall state of fitness, and it can vary as the result of certain infections.

Respiration—The respiratory rate, depth of breathing, and whether any abnormalities can be heard when the chest is listened to with a stethoscope are all significant.

Temperature—The body temperature is typically raised in association with a febrile illness, and should be taken seriously.

the lower jaw, but do not press too hard, as this makes it more difficult to find. Some people prefer to take the pulse from the artery that extends across the inner face of the foreleg, at the elbow. Practice taking the pulse when your horse is well, so you can locate it easily if the need arises.

When the horse has a raised respiratory rate or pulse, veterinary advice should be sought without delay. It is also a good idea to keep it away as far as possible from its fellows to minimize the possible risk of spread of infection. Thanks to antibiotics, however, many diseases that might have been fatal in the past can now be treated with great success.

being a good equestrian

4

Many riders often fail to appreciate just how observant and sensitive horses can be in terms of the world around them. Horses can recognize a change in routine at an early stage, indicating an outing to a show for example, or respond to the slightest shift in muscular pressure from you when out riding. This does not equate directly with intelligence, however, in spite of the fact that horses have large brains relative to their body size, but is really a manifestation of a survival instinct. Failing to detect a slight movement in the grass, for example, could spell the end for an unobservant equid in the wild, faced with a waiting predator. Awareness is their key to survival, and as a rider, you will need to be responsive and appreciate your horse's sensitivity.

choosing a
saddle

There are a number of types of saddle, designed for different purposes. All have evolved from early saddles, which were initially like modified blankets and simply kept the rider's weight off the most sensitive parts of the horse's back. One of most specialized saddles of today, the sidesaddle, is based on a 700-year-old design. Riding sidesaddle was the style favored by ladies of nobility. It demands a saddle that fits perfectly, as any deviation is likely to result in injury to the horse's spine.

General-purpose English saddles, which are widely used by everyday riders, evolved from the jumping saddle. The modern jumping saddle is based on the design of Count Toptani, a Spanish nobleman, and reflects the ideas of Frederico Caprilli, a cavalry officer from Italy. Caprilli advocated that riders should sit forward and shorten their stirrup leathers for the gallop and, when jumping, be in balance with the horse (see box, right).

Construction

The saddle is constructed around a frame called a tree. The tree is usually made mainly of

Different saddles have been designed for specific purposes, such as jumping, as shown here.

wood, but those used for flat racing are made from fiberglass to reduce the weight of the saddle—racing saddles weigh no more than 8oz (0.2kg). The bulk of the saddle is traditionally made of leather, although synthetic substitutes are now commonly available.

Saddle fitting

A saddle must be the correct width and length for your horse, to provide a comfortable fit. Never use a numnah (see p.125) when fitting a saddle.

A saddle's length is measured across the center, from the pommel to the cantle, and is usually given in inches. The most common lengths are 16in, 17in, 17^1/$_2$in, and 18in. Widths are usually called narrow, medium, wide, and extra

Saddle Types and Fitting

Jumping saddles have forward-cut flaps with large knee rolls, and the stirrup bars are also sited in a forward position, allowing for shorter stirrup leathers. The general-purpose saddle has larger saddle flaps and a larger waist, so the rider's weight is more evenly distributed over the horse's back. The dressage saddle has a much deeper seat with straight flaps. This enables a rider to have longer stirrup leathers and, thus, a deeper seat.

Dressage saddle *General-purpose saddle* *Jumping saddle*

Western Saddle

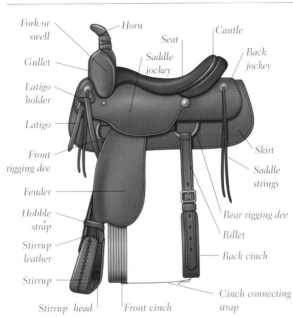

Fork or swell
Horn
Seat
Cantle
Saddle jockey
Back jockey
Gullet
Latigo holder
Latigo
Front rigging dee
Fender
Hobble strap
Stirrup leather
Stirrup
Stirrup head
Front cinch
Skirt
Saddle strings
Rear rigging dee
Billet
Back cinch
Cinch connecting strap

The origins of the western saddle lie in North America, where cowhands spent most of the day riding over large areas attending to their herds of cattle. First and foremost, it needed to have a comfortable design. This was achieved by making sure the seat of the saddle was well padded, and by having the stirrups long, so there was no need for the rider to crouch up on the mount. The horn at the front could be used as a place to wrap a rope to make it easier to move a lassoed steer along. Western saddles are often ornamented with ornate designs carved into the leather.

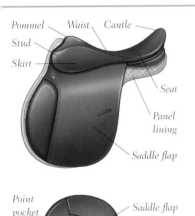

Pommel
Waist
Cantle
Stud
Skirt
Seat
Panel lining
Saddle flap

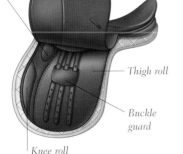

Point pocket
Saddle flap
Thigh roll
Buckle guard
Knee roll

An English saddle must be neither too wide, exerting undue pressure on the spine and withers, nor too narrow, pinching these areas of the body. The correct length is also important. The degree of stuffing is significant, too, because if it needs restuffing, it may well slope down on one side of the body.

FRONT

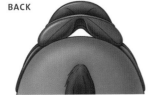

BACK

wide, based on the tree. Your saddler should see your horse to check on the size required. If you are buying a saddle without the help of a saddle fitter, find the width your horse needs by making a template, or wither pattern. This is done by molding a length of reasonably sturdy wire or a "flexi-curve" over his withers and transferring the resulting shape to a piece of cardboard. Cut this out and use it to check the front arch of the saddle. A suitable saddle will have a front arch of the same width and shape.

If the saddle is too wide, it will press down on the withers and spine, whereas if it is too narrow, it will pinch this part of the body. Looking at the saddle from behind when it is on the horse, you must be able to see a clear area running centrally beneath it, and it should be level from front to back, when viewed from the side (see box, left). If the stuffing on the panel causes it to slope more on one side than the other, this can be easily corrected by having the saddle reflocked. This needs to be carried out regularly in any event, even if you purchase a new saddle.

girths
and other saddle accessories

The girth keeps the saddle on the horse's back. Girths are available in various materials in a range of lengths and designs. All girths should be inspected regularly, to make sure the stitching holding them together has not deteriorated. Particularly check the stitching around the buckle.

Leather is the traditional material for a girth; it must be kept clean and supple to prevent it from rubbing and causing soreness (girth galls). The three main designs of leather girth are the three-fold, the Atherstone, and the Balding. Nylon girths made from lengths of cord knotted together with string should be tightened with care since they can also cause chaffing. Webbing girths are not particularly popular because they are not very durable and need to be worn in pairs. All these types of girth must be washed on a regular basis to maintain their flexibility.

Surcingles and breastplates

Where the risk of a girth breaking is high—for example, where your horse is taking part in a cross-country event—a surcingle, or overgirth, may also be fitted. This runs over the

A breastplate serves to prevent the saddle from slipping backward, and comes in the form of a leather strap.

Girths

Girths are traditionally made of leather, although cotton, nylon, and polyeurethane are also used. The girths shown below are mainly leather in various designs. When they are fitted correctly, the buckles on standard girths are sandwiched between the saddle flap and the panel. Here, they cannot pinch the horse's body and are not felt by the rider. Dressage girths are shorter than standard girths since the girth straps on a dressage saddle are very long. This design lowers the position of the girth buckles so they do not interfere with the very subtle leg aids given to the horse by the dressage rider.

Types of girth from left to right: Atherstone, with and without webbing, three-fold, and Balding.

Two designs of dressage girth. An extra tongue of leather protects the horse's body from the buckles.

Safety stirrups are very important to prevent your feet from being trapped if you have the misfortune to fall off.

top of the saddle and the girth, and is held in place with a buckle. Breastplates are used to stop the saddle from slipping backward. They are attached to the front of the saddle by a system of thin straps.

Numnahs

A numnah is a pad, often shaped like the saddle, that fits under the saddle to provide extra comfort for the horse or temporarily to improve the fit of a saddle. Lying directly on the horse's back, it will absorb sweat and must be washed regularly to prevent any risk of soreness. The center of the numnah fits into the gullet of the saddle to avoid pressure on the horse's spine.

Stirrups

The stirrup irons are the rider's foot rests. They are usually made of stainless steel, which is very durable, and some have rubber treads, which give a better grip. Safety stirrups are recommended for younger riders, to avoid the possibility of their being dragged by the horse in the event of a fall. They incorporate a thick rubber band on the outside edge. This will break easily in an emergency, freeing the foot from the stirrup. Check the band at regular intervals, to make sure the rubber has not deteriorated.

It is vital to make sure you have the correct size of stirrup for your feet, to avoid getting stuck or slipping

The Tack Room

Tack is expensive so it is important to look after it properly in a secure tack room. Here, you need individual saddle racks on the walls, as well as bridle hooks. The room also has enough space to clean your tack. Although cleaning is important before a show, it should be carried out on a regular basis, to prolong the life of your tack. Leather, for example, will crack if it is allowed to dry out and the natural oil is not replaced using saddle soap. Some tack, such as numnahs, may be cleaned in a washing machine.

With theft of tack being relatively commonplace, you need to mark your tack so you can identify it easily should it be stolen and then recovered—although in reality relatively little stolen tack is retrieved, and it is more likely that you will need to claim for it on an insurance policy. Most equine policies offer cover for tack, but there are frequently quite strict stipulations about how it should be kept, and if these conditions are not met, any claim is likely to be turned down.

through, either of which is potentially catastrophic. Wearing your usual riding shoes, put your foot into the stirrup. If the stirrup fits properly, there will be a gap of approximately $^1/_2$in (12mm) between your foot and the side of the stirrup on each side.

bridles
and how to fit them

The bridle gives control over the horse's head and, via the bit, enables the rider to steer and brake. Most commonly made of leather, it consists of a number of different components, held together with buckles and hooked billets. The names of the pieces give a good indication of where they fit on the horse. The headpiece loops over the top of the head, behind the ears, with the cheekpieces running down each side of the face and providing the point of attachment for the bit at the lower end. The browband slips onto the headpiece and crosses the face just below the ears. It prevents the bridle from moving backward.

Looped around the back of the cheeks, the throatlash stops the bridle from slipping forward. The noseband runs over the top of the horse's head and is held in place by the browband loops. There are various types of noseband (see box, right); the simplest is the cavesson, which can be used on its own or as an attachment for a standing martingale.

Fitting the bridle

For the horse's comfort and the most efficient rider control, the bridle must fit well. There are three basic sizes: pony, cob, and full. They come in various designs with straps of

---

Types of Bridle

WESTERN BRIDLE
The bridle shown below is one of several that Western riders might use. It is a one-eared rolled bridle with a fixed-cheek curb. The bit looks severe, but it is only used to give the lightest of commands to highly obedient horses.

ENGLISH, OR CLASSICAL, BRIDLE
The snaffle bridle is probably the most commonly used of all bridles. It is designed to be very adjustable so it can be altered to fit an individual horse. It is also safe, and is not easily pulled or slipped off.

A western bridle is designed to achieve a quick response from the horse.

A decorated bridle corresponds with the ornate western saddle style.

Reins allow accurate control, which is vital for maneuverability.

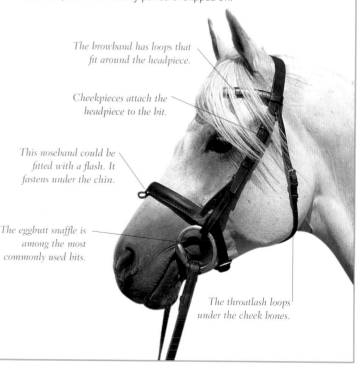

The browband has loops that fit around the headpiece.

Cheekpieces attach the headpiece to the bit.

This noseband could be fitted with a flash. It fastens under the chin.

The eggbutt snaffle is among the most commonly used bits.

The throatlash loops under the cheek bones.

This pony has a flash noseband, which closely resembles the cavesson, but has an extra lower strap above the nostrils, fastening below the bit.

Nosebands

Although the cavesson is more for appearance than function, other nosebands assist the rider in controlling a difficult horse. The drop noseband (below center) is a typical example. It prevents the horse from opening its mouth and crossing its jaws, thereby evading the bit.

The bosal is traditionally part of the bitless bridle used in western riding. The nosepiece, which is the part generally described as the bosal in this case, is made from plaited rawhide and lies about 4in (10cm) above the nose. Both its weight and that of the heel knot under the jaw become lighter as the horse learns to respond to this control.

A drop noseband must be properly fitted to avoid restricting the horse's breathing. When fastened, it rests approximately 4in (10cm) above the nostrils, and is buckled under the chin, in the chin groove. In this position, it keeps the bit in the center of the mouth and exerts pressure on the nose, encouraging the horse to keep its head down.

The grakle works in a similar way to the drop noseband, but has an upper strap, so it restricts the jaw more. The kineton (not shown) does not inhibit movement of the jaw, since there is no backstrap. It is operated by the reins and, when correctly adjusted, exerts pressure on the front of the nose. It can be effective in controlling a horse that pulls.

different widths and with plain or decorated nosebands and browbands. The cavesson and the throatlash are usually undone to fit the bridle, which is slipped over the head, the bit being gently eased into the horse's mouth. The throatlash and cavesson can now be fastened. The cavesson should be buckled so you can fit two fingers between it and the horse's cheekbone. There needs to be roughly a hand's width between the throatlash and the cheeks. If this is the first time the horse has worn the bridle, check the fit of the browband—it must not pull the headpiece forward, which will cause chaffing on the ears— and the lie of the bit in the mouth. (More details about how to put on a bridle are given on p.134.)

bits
and their uses

The bit fits into the horse's mouth and should rest over the tongue. It is very important that it is the right type for your horse, and that it is the correct size. If the bit is too wide for the horse's mouth, it will protrude and the action will be affected. Obviously, if it is too narrow, it will pinch the lips at the corners of the mouth. A thin bit will apply pressure to a restricted area of the tongue, so is considered harsher than a thick one. But a very thick bit may make the horse gag. Check that the tongue fits easily under the bit and that there is plenty of space in the mouth for it: a horse with a narrow nose will need a thinner bit than one with a more generous muzzle.

Dear Equine Casebook

About six months ago I bought a 14.2hh, part-bred Arab, about seven years old. I am quite pleased with him, except when we go out for long hacks, when he can become very difficult, pulling and shaking his head, and generally snatching at the bit. I have tried many different types of bit, but none of them seem to make any difference to his behavior. A friend suggested I try a bitless bridle, but I don't know much about them.
Yours truly, Josie Jones

First of all, you must get your horse's mouth and back checked. It could be that he is in pain and trying to evade the bit to ease the discomfort. If these areas turn out to be fine, you might, indeed, find that a bitless bridle will help. Bitless bridles are commonly used in endurance riding because they are less tiring on the horse's mouth, but also give a greater degree of control over an excited animal. Arabs and part-Arabs seem to have particularly sensitive mouths and often benefit from this type of bridle. The most sensitive parts of the mouth are the tongue and bars.

Choosing a suitable bit, such as this loose-ring snaffle, depends partly on the horse's individual conformation.

There is a very wide variety of bits available, and all work by applying pressure to different parts of the horse's mouth and lips, and in some cases to the head. Most are made of stainless steel, which is very easy to clean, but other options include rubber and nylon, and are not as hard or as cold in the mouth.

The most common bit is the snaffle. It acts primarily on the lips, tongue, and bars of the mouth, although the precise actions differ slightly, depending on the design. The mildest form is the unjointed snaffle, which acts on the ridges on the roof of the mouth. Other common bits include the pelham, which has a curb chain and a bridoon mouthpiece. It was developed as a substitute for the double bridle (see box, right).

Snaffle Bits and How to Fit Them

The choice of a suitable bit is very important. The mildest versions of the snaffle bit are straight and thick, and they are usually recommended for young horses. Most single-jointed bits will have a squeezing action in the mouth. The bit needs to fit so that once it is straight in the horse's mouth, it extends out about a farther ¹/₄in (5mm) on each side. It must not lie so tightly in the corners of the mouth that it causes a distortion here.

When selecting a new bit, it is vital to make sure it fits correctly in the horse's mouth.

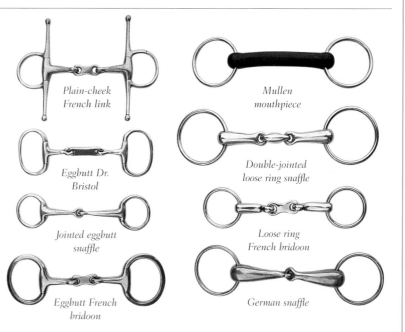

Plain-cheek French link

Mullen mouthpiece

Eggbutt Dr. Bristol

Double-jointed loose ring snaffle

Jointed eggbutt snaffle

Loose ring French bridoon

Eggbutt French bridoon

German snaffle

Bitting problems

There are several reasons why a horse might object to the bit. In youngsters, lack of experience is most likely to be the cause. However, with suitable training and patience, most horses will learn how to respond. Care must be taken to prevent lasting damage to the mouth during the learning process. If the horse is being backed, it will need to adjust to the weight of a rider, and this, too, may affect its ability to cope with a bit.

Poorly fitting bits and dental problems are other causes of resistance in the mouth, as are conformational problems and discomfort in the back.

The pelham is a combination of the bridoon and the curb, positioned lower in the mouth.

Double Bridle

The double bridle is used for more advanced schooling and showing, where precise control and response are very important. As its name suggests, the double bridle incorporates two bits in the form of a bridoon (snaffle) bit, working in combination with a curb bit. The bridoon has its own headpiece and cheekpiece, and lies above the curb bit.

When a horse keeps its head low, in an approximate vertical plain, the bridoon exerts an effect on the bars in the mouth.

Once the horse raises its head, this bit works farther back, toward the molar teeth. This has the effect of stiffening the horse's back area, restricting forward movement from the quarters.

catching
your horse

Horses, with their instinctive curiosity and alertness, soon recognize when you come to their field, often because it means that you are bringing them food. You can build on this when it comes to catching your horse. Make a routine of approaching and patting the horse whenever you enter its field, so that it becomes used to being handled when loose. You can even reward it with treats and groom it.

Catching problems

With a youngster, you should establish your routine from an early age. However, a newly acquired older horse might not respond immediately to you, as it is in new surroundings and you are a stranger. Over time, the bond between you will grow, and it will learn to trust you. In the meantime, however, the worse thing that you can do is to run after the

Dear Equine Casebook

My pony is very naughty about being caught. He waits until I get close to him with the headcollar and then trots off, just out of reach. This is very frustrating, and I can't think of how to stop him. Please help.

Best wishes, Betty Harris

When a horse is reluctant to be caught, it will often move off as you approach, responding to your movements and remaining just out of reach, rather than disappearing off across to the

other side of the field. It is important not to allow him to do this as it will become a habit that is hard to break. You could try getting someone else to help you usher him into the corner of the field, so at least he has not got so much space to run away. Alternatively, try following him gently but persistently, so that he cannot graze. It may take some time, but eventually he may decide to take a step toward you. At this point, walk off. Hopefully, he will start to follow you and, at least on this occasion, the problem will have been overcome.

LEFT: Approach your horse slowly so you do not spook it. Don't flap the headcollar around.

BELOW: Slip the headcollar quickly and smoothly over your horse's head. A well-trained horse will stand still for this.

Dear Equine Casebook

I have a very well-mannered gelding about ten years old. I have owned him for about six months, and he has always been very happy to be caught and ridden. However, recently I went to get him in from the field, and he ran away as if he was scared of me. It took me ages to catch him. What have I done?

Yours truly, Martin Stevens

When a horse that is normally very willing to be caught proves difficult, it may indicate that something has happened to upset it. For example, dogs or even other people wandering through the field could have affected its confidence. It could also be that there was a storm brewing. Horses seem to be able to sense a storm before it starts, and this can affect their behavior. When they are out in a field, horses often find thunderstorms at night upsetting.

horse in an attempt to catch it. Not only will it be able to outrun you, but it may see the running as a game or even a threat. As a precautionary measure, before you let a horse out in the field for the first time, consider putting a headcollar on to make it easier to catch. It is sometimes recommended to attach a short rope—1ft (30cm) or less—to the headcollar. Should you feel that this is necessary, use a length of leather, which will break if caught. The headcollar should also be leather, or designed to break easily.

Most horses can be caught quite easily by means of bribing them with tidbits, but try to avoid falling into this trap if possible. Train your horse to either stand or come to you.

leading
your horse

Being able to lead a horse comfortably and safely is such an important part of its management that this aspect of training must never be neglected. It can make the difference between enjoying the company of the horse and suffering a long catalog of embarrassing and possibly dangerous incidents, whether in the yard or at a show.

Teaching a foal to lead

One of the earliest lessons a domesticated foal has to learn is how to walk on a halter. From birth, a young horse will instinctively follow its mother, and it is this instinct that we make use of when

teaching it to be lead. This should be done while the foal is still comparatively small, rather than when it is a larger and more unruly youngster. A soft foal slip (smooth headcollar) is used. Unlike a halter, it exerts no pressure on the head, which might be actively resented by the young horse.

Start by wrapping a towel around the foal's neck, and then encourage the mare to walk forward, with the youngster following. You can push from behind, if necessary, at this stage. Before long, the foal should be accustomed to moving with the towel, which can be used increasingly for directing its movements, and you can eventually replace the towel with a lead rope. When the foal is moving as you wish, keep the lead rope just slack so there is no pressure on it. If the foal pulls away, the halter will tighten unpleasantly, so it will soon learn not to do this. This is a very important lesson. Encourage the foal when it responds correctly, but do not let it come so close to you that it steps on your feet or makes you stumble. It is vital that its head is level with you at all times—in this position, you will be well away from its feet, whereas if you walk parallel with its shoulder, the horse will be in front and more inclined to pull ahead.

Leading problems

Unfortunately, once the initial stages have been mastered, some owners do not continue with the training, and as a result, especially once the horse is significantly bigger, it may become very difficult to lead. Do not feel intimidated by this. Should the horse start to pull

Horses that are obedient and trustworthy on the lead rope can be enjoyed, safely, by everyone.

An animal that responds well in hand (left) will usually also be a pleasure to ride (below).

ahead, stop and make it back up, assuming the correct position, before setting off again. Be prepared to admonish it if it fails to respond as you wish.

In the case of a strong individual, a chain lead is a safer option than a bridle, which might injure the horse's mouth if it misbehaves. With the lead held between your thumb and index finger, pull on it briefly when the horse starts to tug away from you, and then immediately allow it to slacken off again. The horse should soon realize what is expected of it, and its behavior should improve accordingly.

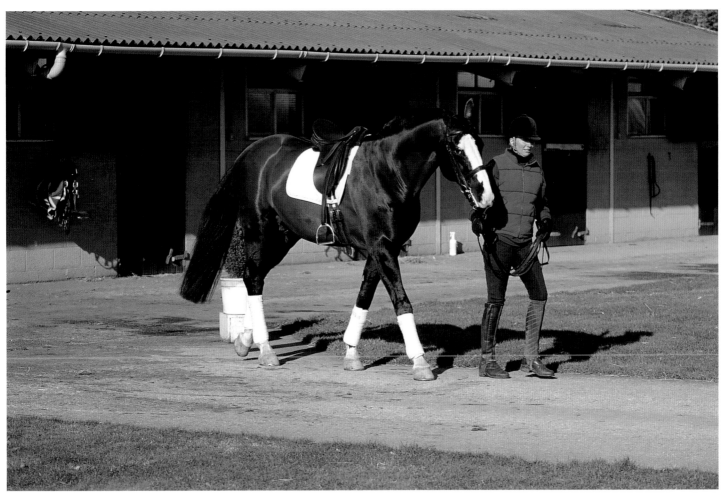

getting ready to
go riding

Before you begin tacking up, make sure you have all the necessary equipment and that it is in good order. Include in this your hat, gloves, riding boots, and any other items you need for riding. Make sure your horse is properly groomed (see pp.84–87) and that its feet have been picked out.

Putting on the saddle

Start tacking up by putting on the saddle. Before you put it on, you should be sure that it is clean, so it will not make the horse's back sore, and that it is in good condition—a worn girth strap is potentially very dangerous. Lift it over the horse's back, and make sure the numnah is properly positioned underneath, without creases under the saddle. Loosely buckle up the girth so the saddle cannot slip.

Putting on the bridle

Once the saddle is secure, you can fit the bridle. Again, you must be sure that all the buckles and billet hooks are safe and check particularly that the bit is clean.

Holding the bridle over your left arm, undo the lead rope and place the reins over the horse's head. Remove the headcollar, using the reins to provide control if necessary.

Preparing to mount

Before mounting, check the girth to make sure it is tight, but not pinching the skin. Check that your riding helmet is firmly in place so it will not slip off when you mount the horse, and that you have the whip held securely in your left hand. It is probably better to wait until you are mounted before carrying out any adjustment to the stirrups.

Step 1—To fit the bridle you must first slip the bit into the horse's mouth using your left hand. A reluctant horse can usually be encouraged to open its mouth by pressing with the thumb just behind the curve of the lips.

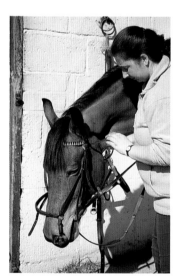

Step 2—Now, with your right hand, slide the headpiece over the horse's head, using your left hand to pull its ears gently through. Ease the forelock over the browband, and make sure the mane lies flat under the headpiece.

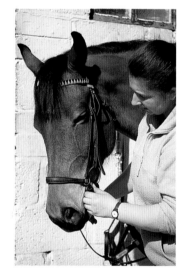

Step 3—Do up the throatlash, making sure you can slip four fingers between it and the horse's cheek-bones, then check that all the parts of the bridle are correctly positioned and not twisted. This could otherwise be painful for the horse.

Step 4—Finally, fit and adjust the noseband. This is a drop noseband, so it should be fitted as described on p.127, so that it does not restrict the horse's breathing. Any badly fitted tack may cause even a good-natured horse to play up.

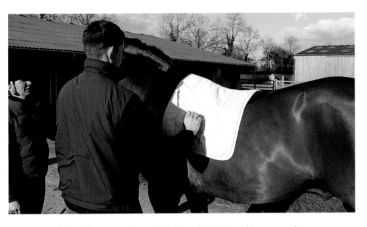

Step 1—Position the numnah on the horse's back, making sure there are no creases and that there is the same amount on both sides of the backbone. Always use a clean numnah; otherwise, you risk making your horse sore.

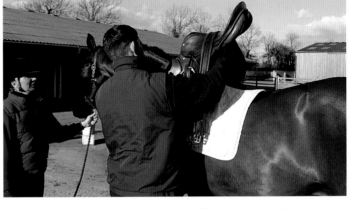

Step 2—Lift the saddle over the numnah. Pull the numnah up into the gullet of the saddle so it does not pull down on the horse's backbone. Never drop the saddle down hard because you risk causing long-term problems.

Step 3—Go to the far side to buckle the girth. Leave it hanging down while you return to the near side where you can reach under the horse's belly to bring it up on the near side of the saddle and fasten it loosely.

Step 4—Before tightening the girth fully, check that there are no wrinkles in the numnah or the horse's skin, particularly near the elbow. Do not tighten it fully until you are ready to mount.

Riding Gear

When riding or working with horses, it is very important to be correctly dressed, for the sake of safety as well as comfort. A riding helmet that conforms to the latest safety standards is absolutely essential. It must fit you properly and will need to be replaced if you fall off. Special riding boots will help you keep a secure grip in the stirrups. Breeches or jodphurs are not vital, but are much more comfortable to ride in than jeans. For jumping, particularly cross-country, you should wear a body protector. It is important to keep warm and not become soaked if it rains while you are out riding. If the weather looks bad, you may decide to wear lightweight waterproof clothing. Gloves are also important, especially when lungeing your horse. Should you be taking part in a competition, you will need to dress according to the context of the event. You will also need to wear a number for identification purposes while competing.

first steps
to riding

Mounting a horse should always take place from the left-hand side (near side), as distinct from the right-hand side (off side). Hold the reins and whip in your left hand, keeping the reins short so the horse does not attempt to move forward. Use your right hand to position the stirrup, so you can place your foot easily into it.

Mounting should be done in a gentle and flowing movement. Place your right hand on the far side of the saddle at the waist, your left one on the mane. Put your left foot in the near side stirrup and hop up, removing your right hand from the saddle as you swing your right leg over the horse's back and down into the far side stirrup. It is helpful to use a mounting block, which raises your position before you start to mount. Alternatively, get someone to give you a "leg-up"—push your bent left knee up, allowing you to mount without using the near-side stirrup.

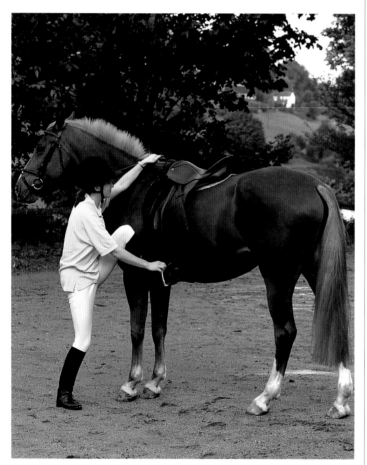

ABOVE: To mount from the ground, use the stirrup for your left leg, placing your left hand on the mane, which will allow you to swing your right leg and body over the horse's back.

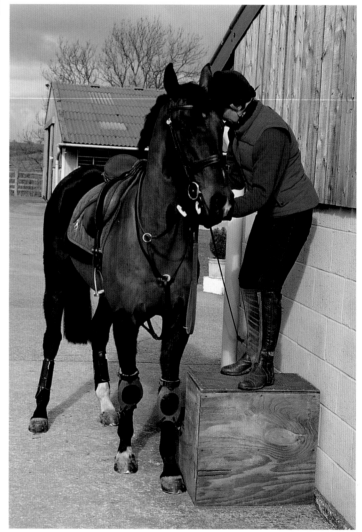

RIGHT: A mounting block can make it easier to get yourself up into the saddle and is less uncomfortable for the horse. Follow the same routine as mounting from the ground.

The hands help to communicate with the horse through the reins, so they must be responsive.

The rider needs to remain alert. With the head up, any problems ahead should be spotted at an early stage.

Adopting correct posture in the saddle improves balance and makes a fall less likely.

It is important to be comfortable in the saddle, and this can be achieved in part by good posture. Exercises, too, can be helpful, to improve the general suppleness of the body.

The lower legs can be used to encourage the horse to move faster if required, as well as helping to control the horse's direction.

The feet can also be used to encourage a reluctant horse to pick up its pace.

BELOW: *The two reins should be held as shown, with a gap of about 4in (10cm) between the hands.*

Dismounting

When you dismount, take both feet out of the stirrups, taking the reins and whip in the left hand. Place your right hand on the front of the saddle, lean forward, and swing your right leg over the horse's back, so you dismount on the near side. Take care not to inadvertently hit the horse while moving your leg across.

Sitting on the horse

Correct posture is vital for all riders. By sitting properly, you allow the horse to perform to the best of its ability, as well as being much more secure in the saddle yourself. When riding normally, sit straight in the saddle, with your

Practice sitting in the saddle to improve your posture. There are also various stretching exercises you can undertake in this position.

weight evenly divided on both sides of the horse. Keep your legs relaxed, because any tension will immediately be transmitted to the horse. The feet should be flat on the stirrup bars, the heels slightly down and the toes pointing almost directly forward.

Picking up the reins

The rein comes from the bit, slots between the last two fingers, crosses the palm, is folded across the side of the index finger, and is held in place with the thumb. The thumbs are always uppermost, with the palms slightly closed and facing inward (see p.137). As the horse walks, its head moves; you should move your arms with the motion of the head, keeping your elbow and hand in a straight line with the rein and the bit.

When you need to hold both reins in one hand, the right rein is usually transferred across to the left hand, where it is held between the second and third fingers, also being restrained by the thumb on top of the index finger.

Communication from the saddle

Riders communicate with their mounts in a number of ways. The movements of your body are very important, as are those of your hands and legs.

To persuade your horse to turn as required, the position of your hands will need to alter. When turning to the left, slacken off on the right rein somewhat, and increase the pressure with your left leg on the girth to institute the turn.

Your legs should be in constant contact with the sides of the horse's body. You can encourage the horse to increase its speed by nudging him with them. They can also be used to direct the horse's hindquarters, by increasing the pressure on one side or the other.

Leg movements are generally combined with the hand signals, via the reins, to communicate what is required. For example, in a well-schooled horse, squeezing the left rein more than the right, while putting more leg pressure on the left side of the body, will result in a turn to the left. Equally, if you sit up in the saddle and give a very slight but even pressure on both reins, a responsive horse will come to a halt, or drop from a trot to a walk.

The voice

Vocal communication plays a part in instructing a horse, with the tone often giving encouragement as well. For example, saying "walk on" will give the horse confidence if it appears slightly unsure of itself. Remember to show appreciation when your horse has responded as you wish, both by patting it on the side of the neck and speaking to it.

Artificial Aids

The voice, legs, hands, and body are called natural aids. Riders may also require artificial aids to encourage a horse to perform. Spurs fit into this category, being worn on the back of the riding boots. They reinforce your leg signals, indicating more determinedly to the horse that it must move forward. The aim is not to cause injury.

WHIPS AND SPURS

The whip is more widely used than spurs, and again it serves to reinforce leg commands. There are a number of different types, with the standard length being about 2^1/$_2$ft (0.74m). The whip is always held at the top and directed downward. The purpose of the whip is not to scare the horse, but to encourage it to behave as required. When it fails to respond to a leg command, repeat the instruction and give a sharp tap at the same time on the area just behind your leg. When you are out in the countryside, a whip can also be used to shut gates behind you, without having to dismount.

TRANSFERRING THE WHIP BETWEEN HANDS

One of the skills that the rider needs to master is transferring the whip from one hand to the other, without alarming the horse by waving it around its eyes. Take both reins into the hand that is holding the whip. Now, with your free hand, pull the whip through the palm and then resume your hold on the reins. A longer whip is passed from one hand to the other by making a semicircle in front of you over the withers.

Whips and spurs are artificial aids that can assist the rider. They should not be used spitefully to punish a horse.

getting to grips with
trot and canter

It helps to be relatively fit for riding; otherwise, you will feel rather stiff afterward, particularly if you ride only occasionally. A supple body is also helpful in communicating successfully with your horse. The upper parts of your body, from the shoulders down through your arms to your hands, are especially important for being in control from the outset. You should also be sitting deep in the saddle as you set off together. Try to relax your mind and body. Horses are very sensitive and will recognize if you are feeling nervous, particularly as this is likely to be transferred through your hands to the reins.

Trot

The need to be in harmony with the horse's movements becomes even more evident once you start to trot. At first, it can be difficult to pick up the rhythm of the rising trot—partly because this is a diagonal pace—but it is largely a matter of getting the timing right. At trot, concentrate on keeping your hands level, and remaining upright and balanced in the saddle, rather than crouching, as the pace becomes faster. Stay alert as well: it is vital to be aware of what is in front of you, in case you need to change direction suddenly. It is important to get into the habit, even while you are learning to trot in a school environment; then, if you meet hazards when you are out hacking, you will be able to cope with them.

Dear Equine Casebook

I have been riding for several months now, and can trot and canter quite well. I am interested in learning how to gallop and would appreciate it if you could tell me a bit about what I should do at this pace.

Best wishes, Lily Gordon

A change of posture is required once you start to gallop. In fact, the stirrup leathers are often shortened for gallop, which makes it easier to lean forward, while still maintaining your balance. By adopting the forward position, you shift your center of gravity back over the horse's center of gravity. Lifting your weight off its back will mean that you do not restrict its movement. Keep your head up and remain alert when galloping because this is a very fast pace, and obstacles can come up very quickly. If you encounter something unexpected ahead, you will have less time to react to it. Be careful where you choose to gallop. Make sure the route is clear, with plenty of space to slow down at the end. Gently ease into gallop from a canter so your horse does not become excited, which may make stopping difficult.

The working trot has two beats to each stride, and at first, it may be helpful to count these beats so you can become familiar with the rhythm. Should this be too slow, it is known as elevated or swimming; if it is too fast, it is called running.

At the canter, you will be able to count three beats. When both the leading fore and hindlegs are on the same side of the body, the canter is described as being either united or true, and this is the most comfortable for riding purposes.

If you are exercising in a school, it becomes quite easy to learn how you need to move, which is by picking up the trotting motion from the horse's forelegs. When the outside front leg (the one closest to the side of the wall or arena) comes forward, you should rise in the saddle, lowering your body down again gently into the saddle when the horse moves this leg back under the body.

Canter

As the pace picks up to a canter, it is important to retain your balance. Avoid tipping forward as this is unbalancing for both you and the horse. On the other hand, you do not want to get "behind the movement," as this means you are tilting backward, behind the horse's center of gravity. The canter rhythm should be gentle, so avoid bumping up and down in the saddle. In trot, the horse's head is still so your hands should be still, but in canter, its head will rock with the beat, so allow your hands to follow this motion.

Four clear footfalls characterize a stride in the case of the gallop, with the horse's stride lengthening as its speed increases. This is the fastest pace, with all four feet momentarily off the ground.

riding
on the road

With more vehicles than ever on the roads, and many drivers being less ready to slow down for horses, the need for training both your mount and yourself for roadwork has never been greater (see p.148). There will probably be a number of occasions, particularly when you are out hacking, that you will need to ride across or along roads with passing traffic, so it is important to make sure your mount is as steady as possible in these surroundings. It is also sensible to avoid riding on a road when the weather is very foggy or after dark, since this is when accidents are most likely. Despite an extensive range of equipment (see right), accidents involving horses are on the increase, emphasizing the need for public liability insurance cover (see p.74).

Dress to be seen

When you are planning to ride on a road, especially for any distance, you need to equip your horse with kneeboots, just in case of a stumble, which can easily happen, especially on minor roads that are not well maintained. It is also important that you are properly dressed to alert drivers to your presence.

Brightly colored retro-reflective equestrian clothing is now widely available, and works by reflecting back the lights from a vehicle. The range includes lightweight polyester tabards embossed with warnings; gloves, which are especially useful for hand signaling if there is a vehicle behind you; and cap covers. Retro-reflective strips around the stirrup irons emphasize the width of the horse and rider, and there are similar leg bands and tail covers for the horse, all held in place with velcro fastenings. As an additional precaution, stirrup reflectors can be used, showing red at the back and white in front. Small, high-visibility safety lights are also available from tack stores.

If you are out riding on an overcast day, particularly near traffic, wear high-visibility clothing to alert drivers to your presence.

Dressed for road riding, this horse has kneeboots with reflective strips and the rider is wearing bright gear. A reflective vest would be a useful addition.

Consider other road users

It is important to show consideration for drivers. For example, if the lane is too narrow for a vehicle to pass you and your horse, do not continue down the road apparently oblivious to the car behind; otherwise, the driver may use the horn in an atttempt to alert you to his presence. Although you should have accustomed your horse to this during training, horns can sound different, depending on the vehicle, and this might distress him. Do not be tempted to speed up if a driver gets too close behind you, particularly since there could be another vehicle coming the other way.

This horse seems very sensible, calmly putting up with all sorts of distractions, but this is a busy road and the rider could have made herself more visible to be on the safe side.

Fact File

Do:
• Wear reflective clothing.
• Put kneeboots on young horses.
• Ride on the correct side of the road.
• Make clear signals of your intentions.
• Wave a thank you to courteous drivers.

Don't:
• Hog the road—ride to one side.
• Ride two or more abreast.
• Ride along chatting and not paying careful attention to other road users.
• Assume that all drivers understand horses.
• Speed up if a car comes up behind you.

When a driver passes you, you may want to pull up your horse's pace, but ultimately it should be confident enough to be able to carry on walking. Finally, remember to take time to thank a thoughtful driver with a wave. It may seem a rather old-fashioned courtesy, but it is always appreciated and emphasizes that slowing down for a horse is a necessary maneuver.

how horses jump

Horses jump instinctively, but in the wild they will normally do so only if they are being pursued by a predator. Jumping is potentially more dangerous than riding on the flat, and it is not something that should be undertaken until you are confident about remaining in the saddle. Wearing a body protector and getting proper instruction are highly recommended. Balance is the key to jumping, and it is not uncommon for novice riders to be unseated as the horse takes off.

Five stages in jumping

There are five recognized stages in jumping (see right). The approach is especially important since, if this is wrong, the horse is unlikely to clear the obstacle. The takeoff follows, with the horse using its strength to leap into the air. There will be a period when it is suspended off the ground as it clears the obstacle, before landing and then getting back into its stride during the final stage, known as the recovery.

Stage 1 - *The first stage in jumping is the approach, which must be right for the horse to clear the obstacle easily. The best approach is a straight line toward the center of the jump. If the pace is too fast, the horse will have difficulty in timing the jump and may get to too close to clear it. Do not to pull on the reins in the last few strides, which will distract the horse and put it off its stride.*

Dear Equine Casebook

I have been riding for about two years and am quite competent, except for jumping. My horse regularly refuses at fences. I have fallen off him a few times because of this, and I am beginning to lose my nerve. In fact, when I approach a fence, I expect my horse to refuse, which he then does. How can I get him out of the habit?
Yours sincerely, Barry Barlow

It is not uncommon for horses to refuse when they feel that the rider is less than certain of the jump. I recommend that you have a few lessons with a good instructor, who will soon be able to tell if the refusal problem is yours or your horse's. If your horse has lost confidence, a few schooling sessions over smaller fences will help to rebuild this. However, if your horse has had a long show-jumping season and is simply stale, it might be best to avoid jumping for a while and concentrate on hacking and fun activities. A horse can become bored simply repeating the same tasks, and it may start to play up as a result.

Stage 2 - *The second stage is the takeoff, when you become airborne. With the hindlimbs tucked up under its body to provide the propulsive power to leap forward, the horse pulls back its neck and lifts its head. The rider adopts a jumping position at the point when the horse's forelegs are lifted. A serious riding fault is to be behind the movement at the takeoff, which will hinder the horse's ability to get over the jump.*

Stage 3 - *When in the air—stage three—the horse stretches forward with its head and neck, which point downward in preparation for landing. Its back is rounded, and first the forelegs, then the hindlegs are tucked up under the body. At this stage, the rider should be looking up rather than down, remaining still in the saddle. If the horse does not lower its head and neck, it may have difficulty clearing the obstacle.*

Stage 4 - *Just prior to landing—stage four—the horse stretches out its forelegs, in preparation for impact. Its forelegs touch down first, one slightly before the other, followed by its hindlegs. At the same time, its head and neck move upward to maintain its balance, while the rider needs to be moving to a more upright position, but still without puting any weight on the horse's back.*

Stage 5 - *The fifth and final phase of the jumping sequence is the recovery, or getaway, and in some cases by this stage, horse and rider will be very close to the next jump, so there is little margin for error. Once its hindlegs have touched down, therefore, the horse needs to get back into its stride and rhythm without delay. At this point, the rider's control is very important in lining up the horse on its approach to the next obstacle.*

learning some
advanced techniques

There are a number of variants that can be developed once walk, trot, and canter have been thoroughly mastered. It is most important that you do not attempt to force your horse to learn the more advanced paces outlined here until both of you have a full grasp of the basic paces. Bear in mind that some horses learn at a faster rate than others, and be prepared to be sensitive to the way your mount responds to schooling and adjust your methods accordingly. While it may be tempting to blame your horse for not doing everything correctly, it may be that you are expecting it to learn too fast.

Collected and extended walk

In advanced schooling, walk is refined into various sub-categories. The collected walk is a slower, more deliberate pace than the medium and free walk. In collected walk, the horse's legs are lifted farther off the ground, but the

strides are shorter, so less ground is covered. This is quite a difficult pace to achieve, since horses are often reluctant to shorten their stride.

On the other hand, one of the characteristics of the extended walk is an increase in pace, with the strides themselves also being lengthened. In extended walk, the hind feet will land beyond the hoof prints made by the

In the case of the medium trot, a horse takes longer steps than during the working trot and moves at an increased speed.

During the extended walk, a horse covers as much ground as possible.

The extended trot is the fastest of the trotting paces, with the feet reaching consistently forward, without then being drawn back.

front feet. The aim in this pace is to increase speed through extending the stride, not, as happens with many horses, just to move faster.

Changing paces in the trot and canter
Equivalent changes in stride length can also be taught for in trot and canter. In addition, however, there is also a medium pace, which lies between the usual working pace and the extended one. In medium trot, for example, the horse should have a longer stride length, thus covering more ground, but the rhythm, as well as the tempo, must not differ from that of the basic trot. Until the horse has mastered these movements, loss of balance can be a problem in achieving the correct rhythm.

Lateral Movements

Lateral, or sideways, movements increase the horse's responses to the rider, as well as improving its balance and suppleness. Teaching lateral movements can begin very simply in the yard or stable while you are on the ground. Simply lean on the horse's body, in the area of the girth, to persuade it to step sideways. Once it has learned to do this with the minimum of pressure, the next stage is to teach it to turn on the forehand. This is when the back legs step a semicircle around the inner front leg, by repeatedly crossing over each other. This movement is very useful when out hacking because it allows you to position the horse easily for opening and shutting gates without dismounting. Start training for this maneuver in front of an obstacle; then there is no risk of the horse's attempting to move forward unexpectedly.

The ability of horses to master these more complex movements depends partly on the individual. The most highly schooled horses in dressage can make a full pirouette, through 360 degrees, at a canter.

Shoulder in often features in dressage tests. During this action, the horse moves forward at an angle.

Haunches in to the center of the school indicates the movement known as travers, carried out at the trot.

Half pass entails crossing of the outside legs in front of the inside legs, usually at a trotting pace.

teaching a young horse
about traffic

Teaching a horse that traffic poses no significant danger is a long-term process, and it helps to accustom even a relatively young foal to the sights and sounds of cars and other vehicles in the yard, perhaps by leading it past with its mother. You may also be able to turn a youngster out in a field adjoining a road, with a mature companion, where it will have the opportunity to become accustomed to the noise of traffic. Once the horse is broken, ride through puddles occasionally, so that water splashes its legs, like a passing car will do on wet days.

When you venture out on a quiet road for the first time, lead the youngster on the right-hand side of the road, as you would if riding it. Take a light schooling whip and use this to keep it straight, flicking at its hindquarters if necessary. If your horse proves very nervous, take a steady companion along and get this horse to walk on the outside, nearest the traffic. Do not let your horse become too reliant on having company, however, since ultimately it will

Dear Equine Casebook

I have been working with a youngster for the past few months and have recently backed her with no problems at all. She is quite bold in the school and also fairly relaxed. We have begun short rides on the road, and she is relatively good with traffic, but she seems to be afraid of tractors. Please could you tell me how I can persuade her that they are not going to hurt?
Regards, John Tucker

This is an awkward situation because, although the tractor driver is likely to be more sympathetic to your predicament than many car drivers, many horses do dislike tractors, partly because they see relatively few of them and partly because they are noisier and wider, and may need to pass closer. On the next few occasions that you meet a tractor, pull in at a convenient spot and let the tractor come by, so your horse can see it more clearly, before riding on. In this sort of situation, it is very important not to send the wrong message to your horse by keeping the reins short, which will suggest there could be a problem ahead, but equally, have firm control of the right side of its body, to make sure it continues to walk in a straight line on the shoulder.

It is well worth teaching a foal at an early age that horse trailers are not a threat, encouraging it to walk up the ramp readily. This is partly because it is much easier to overcome a young horse's reluctance at this age, because it can be persuaded to enter the vehicle more easily than an adult horse, especially with its mother nearby. Repeat this training regularly until the foal will enter by itself.

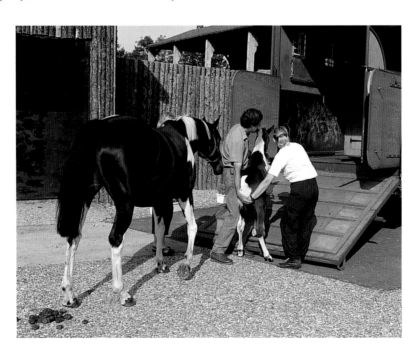

Road Sense

Horses do not instinctively have any road sense, but they can be taught to overcome their fear of traffic. This is an important skill to teach your horse even if you do not intend to ride on the road, because horses do sometimes escape or they may be deliberately released from fields, and they can then run amok in traffic, which will be very dangerous for all concerned. Do not neglect to take out at least third-party insurance, just in case your horse does become involved in an accident.

need to gain the confidence to walk alone. When signaling to traffic, be careful to use the hand without the whip. Otherwise, this is likely to upset your horse and could even catch it in the eye.

The first ride

When you start to ride your horse on a road for the first time, choose the location and time carefully. Although proper riding equipment must be worn at all times, a secure helmet and back protector are especially important when taking an untried horse on the road, to protect you from injury—if you are thrown off, you are almost certain to land on a hard surface.

Follow the route that your horse has become accustomed to walking, which will give it confidence, and aim to go only a short distance. Setting off early on a summer's morning, when you are unlikely to encounter a lot of traffic, is a good idea.

Fact File

- Tell someone where you are going and when you expect to be back.
- Ideally, put protective and reflective gear on your horse and yourself (see pp.142–143).
- Aim to go for a short distance without too many challenges.
- Take a companion, if it's the youngster's first trip.
- Take a schooling whip to guide the horse's movements.
- Consider taking a cellphone, but if you think you will have trouble, spend more time schooling before you venture out.

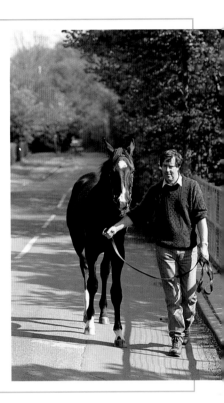

It helps if you can train your horse at first with the assistance of a friend, who will drive past as shown, allowing you to develop your horse's road sense. However, not all drivers will be sympathetic and pass slowly.

Always acknowledge a driver's patience by thanking them with a wave. You should also make sure your horse is properly equipped to be out on the road, unlike the horse in the box at the top of the page.

riding
a young horse

It may seem ideal to start with a young horse that you break and school yourself, in this way making sure it is free from vices and other behavioral problems. However, this is rarely the best route to take unless you have plenty of experience with a variety of horses: it is definitely not to be recommended if you are a relative newcomer to riding. Not only are there many potential pitfalls along the way, but bringing on a youngster is also a fairly lengthy process, meaning that it could be months before you are able to ride on a regular basis, and years before it is able to do all that you wish. There is also the cost to consider, especially if you keep the animal at a livery yard.

Dear Equine Casebook

How does a foal become used to actually being ridden ?
Yours sincerely, Eliza Dunn

The breaking process, known as backing, starts with the rider simply lying across the saddle. The horse is led up and down slowly several times, so it becomes used to the rider's weight. After several days of this, the rider can mount cautiously, without placing their feet in the stirrups, while the young horse is still on a lead rein. Subsequently, it is a matter of walking normally, although the horse should still be led. Recently broken horses are more likely to be nervous than experienced mounts, and they need to be ridden with care.

What You will Need

A lunge rein is an essential piece of equipment for backing purposes. It should be at least 20ft (6m) in length, and attaches to a lungeing caves-son, which is basically a head collar with a noseband. The horse will also need to become accustomed to wearing a mouthing bit at this stage for some time each day. Before long, it will learn to associate the movements of the cavesson with those of the bit. To accustom the horse to the feel of the girth, a breaking roller is used. This needs to be padded and must fit correctly, so that it will not slip if the horse tries to buck it off. The breaking roller is usually held in place with a breastplate, which can be removed once the horse allows the roller to be tightened without bucking. In due course, the horse can be introduced to the saddle and is then lunged with the saddle on (see box, right).

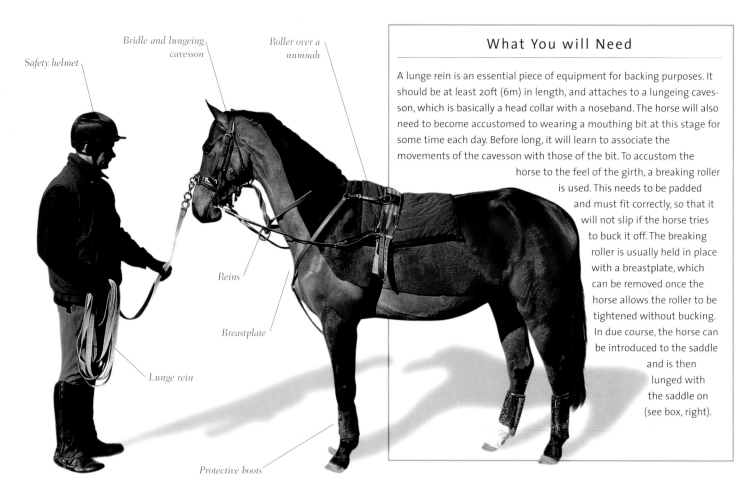

Safety helmet

Bridle and lungeing cavesson

Roller over a numnah

Reins

Lunge rein

Breastplate

Protective boots

Starting a Young Horse

Horses learn at different rates, but it is important to carry out regular training sessions lasting relatively short periods, so you can maintain your horse's concentration. Avoid over-working, which can lead to health problems, with lungeing for example placing stress on a horse's body. Make sure all tack fits properly, making adjustments as required, since this can otherwise cause discomfort or even injury to a growing horse.

Step 1—*Lungeing is a starting point for a young horse being schooled, so it can grow used to the feel of the saddle on its back. At first, it is likely to kick and buck, but this phase will pass quite quickly.*

Step 3—*When the horse is going well, you can mount fully. Ride around gently with someone holding on to the lead rope. This gives the young horse no opportunity to take off and start bucking, and provides closer control than lungeing.*

Step 2—*The next step is to increase the weight on the horse's back, rather than trying to mount up into the saddle. By leaning across the saddle this way, you can escape danger easily if the horse starts to behave badly.*

Step 4—*Once the horse has accepted being ridden and is used to the weight and feel of a rider on its back, you can then start lungeing again, this time with the rider in the saddle.*

Making a start

If you are determined to obtain a youngster, find someone with experience who can guide you. Alternatively, you may want to send the foal away to someone who is used to training young horses for the saddle. Before your horse is ready to be ridden, it is very important to get it used to being caught and handled (see pp.130–31). Horses mature at different rates. For example, if you have a Thoroughbred, you might begin breaking in and schooling at just a year old, whereas another breed may need to be left until it is three. Arabs are notoriously late developers, often not being ready until they are five or even six.

behavioral problems

5

Behavioral problems, varying from aggression toward people to stable vices, are not uncommon in horses. However, it is often possible to overcome them successfully, sometimes simply by making changes in the horse's routine and environment. Remedial training can also be helpful. Luckily, today, there is plenty of help and advice available for dealing with a variety of difficulties. Just as with most physical illnesses, it is best to seek assistance as soon as possible. Ignoring the problem will not make it go away, and may give it time to become habitual. It is worth remembering that it will be far quicker and, therefore, cheaper to treat a problem if it is caught early, than if it has become an ingrained habit.

head-shy and
nervous horses

Horses are instinctively nervous by nature. In some individuals, this nervousness is manifested in such a way that it creates great difficulties in day-to-day management. Take the example of a head-shy horse. Virtually every routine procedure, including grooming, tying up, and riding, will be a challenge, with the horse constantly moving its head away from you.

Again considering a head-shy horse, the reasons for its actions may be that it has not had enough contact with people to get used to being touched, or it could be that it has been deliberately hit around the head in the past, making it very wary of any new approach. Before you start working on the head-shyness, it is well worth consulting a vet, particularly if the horse has only recently started

Horses may only misbehave under certain circumstances, as here, when the owner is trying to administer a dewormer. Holding the head down will assist in this case.

Dear Equine Casebook

I have a Thoroughbred-cross who is five years old, and he is generally going very well. He behaves impeccably in the school and is now beginning to show a real talent for jumping. Unfortunately, when we go hacking, he gets very nervous and leaps at the slightest thing, especially plastic bags, so I can't relax and enjoy myself at all.
Please help, Arthur McCartney

Flapping objects, such as bags caught in bushes, can be very upsetting to a nervous horse. Don't worry, though, there are ways to increase your horse's confidence.

DESENSITIZATION
Get hold of a large sheet of plastic to desensitize him with. First, wrap it around your hand and then gently rub it over his body. Do this slowly and repeatedly so that he becomes used to the sight and sound of plastic. Remember to give him plenty of encouragement. Now, open the sheet out and shake it slightly, not too far away from his head, before folding it up again. Should he show any signs of distress during this stage, do not carry on unfolding, but stop and repeat the first stage again. Always proceed slowly and with patience. A number of short sessions of this type should soon overcome this problem.

behaving this way. Many apparent behavioral problems have an underlying medical cause. A painful neck, soreness in the mouth, or a painful tooth can all lead to a dislike of being touched around the head. If something amiss is discovered, veterinary treatment should resolve the problem without further worry.

Once you are sure that head-shyness is the true cause, you should deal with it directly. Do not be deterred by the horse's constantly pulling away. Start by offering it a treat in your hand (keeping this flat as always), and then slide your hand up around the horse's face, patting it gently and talking to it calmly. Repeat this several times as necessary to build up your horse's confidence.

If all else fails, the use of a pressure halter may be necessary (see box, right). This will encourage your horse to move on your command, rather than hanging back or pulling away.

Pressure Halter

A pressure halter is a means of encouraging a horse to go forward. It consists of a rope halter attached to a lead rope. The horse is persuaded to go forward by the lead rope. If it is reluctant to do so, this causes the halter to tighten over the horse's poll, creating pressure. Although effective, a pressure halter must be used carefully. Keep constant pressure on the lead rope when the horse refuses to go forward, and release the pressure as soon as it moves as required, giving words of encouragement. It is useful for young horses, but also for older ones that do not respond well to a halter.

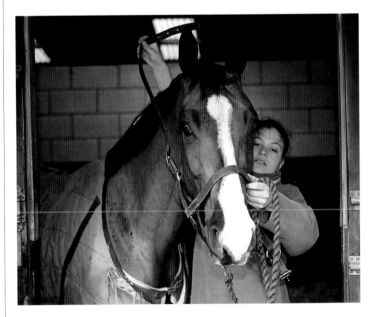

If your horse is head-shy and rears away from you, start by encouraging it to lower its head by offering tidbits from your hand while you stroke the side of its face.

This should then allow you to be able to put on a head collar without your horse trying to escape your hands by pulling its head away.

what are
stable vices?

A stable is an unnatural environment for a horse, so it is not surprising that being kept in one can lead to medical and behavioral problems. Stable vices are common, with affected horses showing what are known as stereotypic patterns of behavior, which are constantly repeated. Although they are called vices, there is no ill-intent on the horse's part, and this sort of problem has been likened to the compulsive-obsessive disorders that can afflict people.

What causes the problem?

Equine behaviorists often classify vices into distinct categories—for example, oral problems, such as chewing, and abnormal movements, such as weaving—but recent studies have revealed a common link, reflected by changes in blood chemistry. Affected horses have raised levels of endorphins. These are opiates, produced naturally in the body, and they make the animal feel good. It is believed that horses become addicted to endorphins, so they continue their abnormal behavior, which may initially have been triggered by a physical cause. A dramatic illustration of the part played by endorphins was shown when a group of seven horses were treated with drugs that blocked the actions of this narcotic. Crib-biting ceased in all cases within 20 minutes—previously some of the horses had been biting their stable doors up to 15 times per minute. In some cases, the effects of this treatment lasted for days.

By watching your horse regularly, you should detect signs of behavior that may develop into vices, such as chewing a chain on the stable door. Take rapid action to prevent it from becoming an habitual problem.

An antiweaving grille lessens the accessible area over the stable door and restricts the horse's ability to move its head, but it will not actually resolve this abnormal behavior.

Boredom can be a contributory cause to the development of stable vices, and it is therefore a good idea to offer your horse a suitable stable toy to play with if it has got to be confined for long periods.

Horses are naturally curious, and their playful natures mean that they will soon start to play with toys provided for them.

Avoiding vices

Boredom plays a part in stable vices, but the underlying cause is often more closely related to the management of the horse. It is important to keep horses outside whenever possible, suitably protected against the cold as necessary. This not only allows them to graze, but also allows for their natural social interactions. While they are stabled, it is possible to ease or avoid vices by using one of the variety of toys designed for this purpose.

Coping with vices

Like all addictions, vices are very difficult to treat successfully. Although its repetitive behavior can be very irritating, there is absolutely no point in punishing the horse for

doing it. In fact, punishment may even make the situation worse, by triggering the release of more endorphins, which also serve as natural painkillers.

Alterations to the horse's environment, such as putting an antiweaving grille on the stable door, may make it harder for a horse to engage in behavior of this type, but they will not offer any long-term cure. The use of certain drugs, notably tranquilizers and antidepressants, may offer some relief, and giving a supplement of the amino acid l-tryptophan, which is important in brain chemistry, has proved beneficial in certain instances. Complementary treatments, notably acupuncture (see p.159), may also help in treating some stable vices. Your vet will be able to refer you to a specialist in this area if necessary.

Wind-sucking horses can be fitted with special collars, as shown here, to try to restrict their habit of gulping air.

Crib biting and wind sucking

Some horses could be more susceptible to behavioral problems, notably those with naturally low levels of endorphins. These are usually released during activities such as grooming, but if the level of release is low or the receptors are less responsive than normal, the horse may try to find ways to increase the effect, which could lead to stable vices, which, as described above, are addictive.

Investigations in this area have also challenged other established thinking. Crib biting is where the horse bites a piece of wood, such as its stable door; it is called wind sucking when the horse grips the wood and then appears to suck in air. It used to be thought that this behavior gave rise to colic, because of the swallowed air. Studies have shown that this is incorrect, as no air actually reaches the stomach. Instead, it only travels a short distance down the gullet. The characteristic noise that accompanies wind sucking is caused by air entering the gullet. It seems that

this behavior simply prevents the horse from eating properly, and it is this that causes the colic. There are other health problems associated with crib biting and wind sucking, notably the wear imposed on the incisor teeth at the front of the mouth. This can be so excessive that the horse finds it difficult to graze. Worse still is the fact that, by this stage, turning the horse out in a field may no longer provide a solution. It may simply carry on crib biting or wind sucking, choosing a new site, such as a gate or a

Allowing a horse as much time out of its stable, turned out into a field, is recommended as a general way of helping to counteract stable vices.

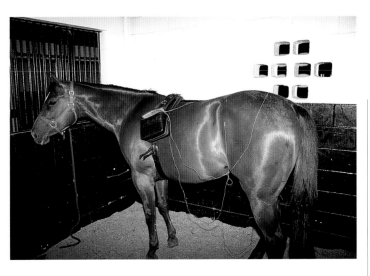

Acupuncture has given good results in some cases in correcting vices. Veterinarians interested in complementary medicine are best placed to advise on the likely value of this treatment.

Domestic Problem

Vices have not been observed in wild equids in their natural habitats. However, when Przewalski's horses are stabled, a high proportion of them will suffer, exceeding the typical figure of around 15 percent seen in their domestic counterparts. Studies on wild herds have confirmed just how active wild horses can be, with Przewalski's themselves typically grazing for more than half a day, being actively on the move for about 2¹/₂ hours during this period. In contrast, if a domestic horse spends barely an hour daily out of its stables, it is not really surprising that, when problems do arise, they are most likely to be encountered in this environment.

fence post. Some horses can progress to wind-sucking through simply arching their necks, without having to grip an object. A special collar, which makes arching the neck difficult, can help to alleviate this problem.

The list of possible abnormal behaviors that can be seen in the stabled horse is large. Some, such as licking the lips, are not immediately indicative of a vice developing, whereas others, such as self-mutilation, where the horse starts to bite itself, are obviously problematic.

RIGHT: The teeth of crib biters will be worn unevenly and need regular attention from an equine dentist.

problems with
the blacksmith

A horse that is difficult to shoe or dislikes having its feet touched is very frustrating. Shoeing is a routine necessity for most horses, and even if you decide to keep your horse without shoes, it will still need regular foot care. If you have a youngster, concentrate on teaching it to pick up its feet from a very early age, rather than waiting until later in its life, when it will find learning much more difficult. If you have acquired a horse that is nervous of the blacksmith, it may simply never have become accustomed to having its feet picked up. On the other hand, it could be that it has had a bad experience in the past. Unfortunately,

unless you can talk to its blacksmith before buying, you will not usually be aware of this until it is too late. Whatever the cause, you will have to try to overcome it.

Correcting behavior at the blacksmith
Although most blacksmiths are sympathetic, they do not have infinite time to wait to carry out their work. If your horse plays up very badly on the first visit, therefore, it is best to abandon the attempt. Book another appointment and arrange for your vet to sedate the horse, which should make shoeing easier. Sedation may also help the horse to

RIGHT: Work on getting your horse to pick up its feet as a matter of course. This will not only make it much easier for you, but also should mean less difficulty when your horse needs its feet attended to by a smith.

BELOW LEFT: Arrange for your horse to be present when other horses are being shod. It can help to prevent a horse from becoming nervous about this procedure.

Twitching

Twitching should not be used as a routine method of persuading a horse to be shod, but it might help in the early stages when you are trying to get it to accept having its feet handled. In other circumstances where a more positive restraint is needed, a twitch can be useful. The twitch is wrapped around the nose where it causes pain, resulting in the release of natural painkillers, called endorphins. It seems that these reduce the horse's desire to lash out. The maximum time that a horse should be twitched is between 10 and 15 minutes, after which it may show signs of aggression, particularly when released from the twitch. This is probably because the endorphins start to lose their effect. If the horse is twitched for no longer than this period, it should not resent the process in the future, but otherwise, it is likely to react badly if a further attempt is made to apply the twitch.

overcome its fear, although it is obviously not a long-term solution. You could try other ways of soothing your horse in preparation for the blacksmith. For example, use a calming feed supplement—there are many on the market—or try complementary treatments, such as Bach's Rescue Remedy.

If you know that your horse is likely to be difficult with the blacksmith, make an appointment at a time when you will not have to rush off if it overruns. Hurrying creates a tension that is likely to be transmitted to the horse, worsening the situation. Also consider booking a longer session than usual, and when the blacksmith comes, stay with the horse to emphasize that there is nothing to fear. In between visits from the blacksmith, work on encouraging your horse to pick up its feet. You may also be able to arrange for it to witness a cooperative individual being shod, since this, too, could help to allay its fears.

Change your blacksmith

If you make no progress, consider trying another smith, possibly one of the opposite sex. It might be that your current smith reminds your horse of someone to whom it took a dislike, for whatever reason, earlier in its life.

dealing with
aggressive horses

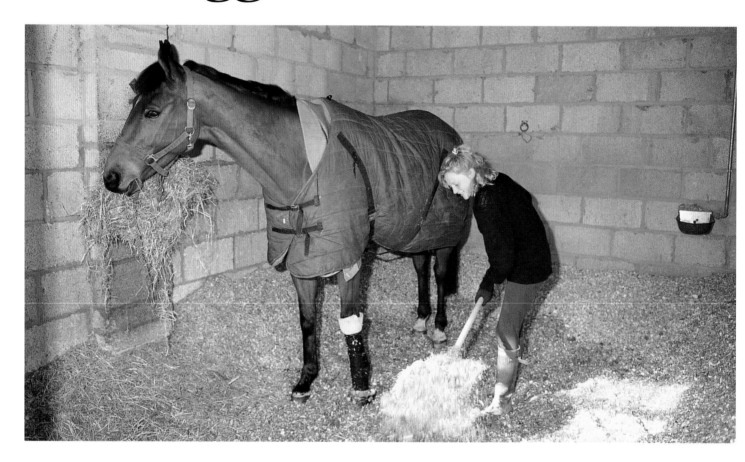

Horses can sometimes be aggressive toward people, which, in view of their size and strength, is potentially very serious. Temperament can be significant in this respect, with Thoroughbreds, for example, being much more likely to lash out than the generally easygoing cobs. It is important to get to know your horse, so you are aware of what is likely to upset it and what it is not worried about. There are certain obvious precautions you can take from the start. For example, take care when grooming a sensitive area, because if you accidentally hurt your horse, this might lead to an aggressive response. Similarly, never approach your horse from behind, where its blind spot is. This could frighten it, which might be dangerous.

Stable precautions

Take care when entering a confined space, such as a stable, because your horse is more likely to react badly when there is no means of escape. Particular care is needed when you are entering a foaling box. Bear in mind that even normally docile mares can become very combative if they feel that their youngster is in danger, and avoid moving between the foal and its mother.

At all times, move slowly and deliberately around the stable, keeping within your horse's field of vision. It can help to establish an organized routine when working with a horse in its stall. This will allow it to learn what you are going to do next, which will give it confidence and make it

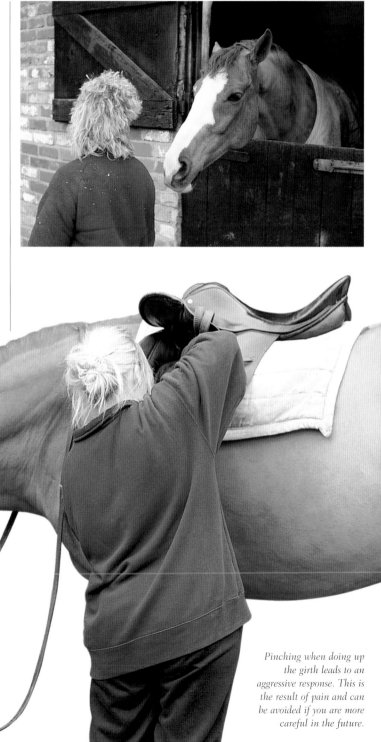

LEFT: A hay net can serve as a distraction for a horse when you have to attend to its needs in a stable.

RIGHT: Stabled horses that nip when you pass are attention-seeking and may have been fed too many tidbits.

Dear Equine Casebook

The other day a friend asked me to muck out his horse and see to its feed. I was happy to do this, until I got into the stable. His normally friendly mare pulled horrible faces at me and put her ears back. She also kicked out at the back wall of the stable. I was quite scared, but managed to get out safely. How can I prevent it happening again?

Regards, Susannah Mapleson

If you find yourself trapped in a stable in a potentially difficult situation, you may be able to make the horse back down by behaving in a dominant way, mimicking the sort of body language that is common in herd power plays, where an established herd member might bully a newcomer, for example. Stand tall and hold your arms out away from your body, which will make you look bigger. Maintain eye contact with the horse and step slightly in its direction, rather than backing off. Speaking in a loud voice can also help. If all else fails, give the horse a sharp tap on the nose—this area is very sensitive in horses. Avoid being caught in this way again by making sure the horse is out of the stable in the future if possible.

feel relaxed. Should you need to provide a diversion, offering a hay net can be useful.

If you notice a decided change in temperament, with the horse being more excitable than normal, consider a dietary cause, with crushed oats in particular having gotten a reputation for having this behavioral effect.

Pinching when doing up the girth leads to an aggressive response. This is the result of pain and can be avoided if you are more careful in the future.

how to cope with
bucking

One of the most common fears among novice riders is that their mount will buck and they will fall off. Bucking is a natural part of a horse's behavior, and may occur when it is excited or scared; it is also a feature of rodeo events, where an unbroken horse is actually encouraged to buck and throw the rider off its back. Really vigorous bucking of this sort is more common among inexperienced youngsters, and once a horse has got used to being ridden, it will tend to be far less dramatic. Nevertheless, novice riders are at greatest risk of being thrown, simply because they do not have enough riding experience to cope.

Staying on a Bucking Horse

Since bucking is rarely related to misbehavior on the part of the horse, seeking to punish the animal when it bucks is unlikely to be effective. Even so, it is important to be able to cope with a bucking horse when you are in the saddle. If you suspect that your mount is going to buck, sit up and use the reins to keep its head up—it will only be able to buck successfully if it can bend its neck downward. With a confirmed bucker, plan your hacks so you go uphill first. Horses cannot position themselves to buck when going up a slope. By the time you return from your ride, your mount should feel sufficiently exercised not to try to unseat you on the way home. Some behaviorists, such as Monty Roberts, can offer help in curing confirmed buckers.

Bucking can often be the result of high spirits, especially in the case of a competition horse, which senses the excitement in the arena.

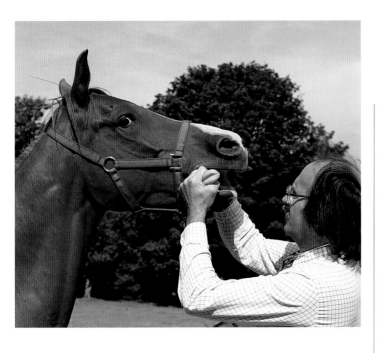

If your horse is not normally a bucker, it could be bucking because it is in pain. Get its teeth and back checked.

Pain as the cause

Even a relatively placid horse may buck when it is in pain, which is why it is always important to double-check that its tack is properly fitted before mounting. Something as simple as a crumpled numnah can cause discomfort and is easily remedied. More difficult is a poorly fitting saddle. Never ride with a badly fitted saddle, which can cause saddle sores and other injuries, which again could be a cause of bucking. If there is no obvious problem, it could be that there is localized pain in other parts of the body, such as the neck, back, or even teeth. If a horse that has rarely bucked before starts to do so, this is one of the most likely causes and needs to be investigated by your vet.

Too little exercise

Poor management may also be a reason for bucking. A horse that is not receiving enough exercise may buck when taken out riding. Lungeing before riding may be helpful in taking the edge off its high spirits. It is also worth turning it out into a paddock for longer periods during the day. Its diet may also need reviewing—a ration that is too high in concentrates, especially crushed oats, can cause problems.

Rearing

Rearing is much more dangerous than bucking because the horse can fall over backward onto its rider. Even experienced riders find it very difficult to cure a confirmed rearer. Never consider buying a horse that is known to rear. Again, rearing can be caused by pain, so if your horse starts rearing for no apparent reason, have its teeth and back checked. If your horse is apparently healthy, however, and yet continues to rear this way, you will need to take effective action. Always start by slackening off your grip on the reins, because you cannot balance with them, and pulling back could easily cause you to fall, dragging the horse down on top of you. One suggestion, if someone is closeby in the arena, is to slap the vulnerable underside of the horse's body with a damp towel, to bring it down rapidly to the ground.

preventing **bolting**

When your horse starts to bolt, pulling hard on both reins together is not likely to be effective, because the horse's strength will be much greater than yours.

Dear Equine Casebook

A friend of mine nearly had a nasty accident recently when his horse took fright and bolted as he was bringing it in from the field. Luckily, she stopped by her stable and no harm was done, but could you tell us how to cope with this in future?
Yours sincerely, Mark Morgan

In this situation, the horse's strength means that you will lose the tug of war and have to relinquish your grip. Try to steer it into a safe area first, so that it cannot run out across a busy road, for example. By doing some groundwork, such as getting the horse to react instantly to pressure on its headcollar, you may be able to prevent a recurrence in the future.

Some riders worry that their horse will run off out of control, taking them with it. Within a herd of horses, bolting, or at least running off, is a common defensive mechanism, allowing the group to escape from danger. Thankfully, however, it is quite unusual when a horse is being ridden, although certain types of horse may be more prone than others. For example, Arabs and other horses bred and kept for racing can run great distances at speed.

Running off in youngsters

The risk of bolting behavior coming to the surface in domestic stock is greatest in young horses. Their inexperience of the world means that they are likely to panic more quickly than older ones. When taking a youngster out on a

A rider needs to stay in the saddle to regain control of a bolting horse. Otherwise, the situation can become very dangerous for all involved.

hack, you need to be alert and watchful; even a large dog with which the horse is unfamiliar can provoke this type of reaction. Bolting is more likely if you are already traveling at speed, so you need to recognize any potential danger spots and be prepared to act swiftly to avoid problems.

Draw your body back, sitting up in the saddle, if you suspect that the horse is going to bolt. Do not crouch forward in the saddle, which is likely to worsen the situation. Try to steer the horse away from whatever has frightened it, and head for open ground, avoiding fences, ditches, or other obstructions that increase the likelihood of your falling off. If you manage to stay aboard, your horse will soon tire and will want to slow down—at this stage, show you are in control by urging it to continue galloping for a period.

Confirmed bolters

Should the horse have a reputation for taking off, you may have prior warning through the reins. Be alert to this, and if you feel that it is about to go, pull sharply and repeatedly on one rein. This makes the horse flex its neck and makes it slow down.

It also unbalances it, which makes it slow down.

Careful schooling and dietary changes can help to cure confirmed bolters. In some cases, however, the inexperience of the rider enables the horse to accelerate out of control.

A bolting horse can be slowed down by being forced to turn in a circle, pulling on just one of the reins.

where and how to
get help

With growing interest in the field of equine behavior, it is becoming increasingly easy to get expert advice on a wide variety of problems. However, it is still a good idea to start with an experienced vet, who will check your horse for signs of illness or pain, which can underlie a number of problems. Your vet should also be able to advise you on the best person to contact in your area, if you do need to consult a behaviorist. If your vet refers you to a behaviorist, the basic costs of the consultation may be covered by your equine insurance. Check the small print in your policy to find out the best way to proceed.

Do not delay in seeking assistance if you think that your horse could have a behavioral abnormality. It is very much easier to deal with this type of problem in its initial stages, before it develops into a chronic habit, after which it will be harder to treat successfully. One thing you can almost guarantee is that the problem will not go away of its own accord. It may even worsen without help, and you will be putting your horse through unnecessary trauma.

Keeping records

One of the key elements for a vet or behaviorist is to know the full history of the animal. Before a consultation, spend some time making notes covering such details as when, where, and how you acquired the horse, its feeding and management, and its age. Also write down exactly when you first noticed the signs you are concerned about, and whether any alterations in the horse's environment occurred at the same time. Include any other factors you think may have been involved in its change in character.

LEFT: It is often easier to keep control of a horse indoors in a riding school, partly because there will be fewer distractions here. Seek advice at an early stage if you encounter a problem.

ABOVE: Outdoors, horses are more likely to be exposed to unexpected noises, such as vehicle horns or thunder, which may upset them. Try to identify possible causes if your horse behaves badly.

In spite of everything, most horses give their owners many years of both companionship and enjoyment, with few worries along the way.

Next steps

Under most circumstances, the vet or behaviorist will need to visit the horse to see it in its usual surroundings and get a full understanding of the problem. If you have a video camera, it is well worth trying to film your horse as it exhibits the unusual behavior, just in case it fails to replicate it when the vet or behaviorist is with you. Your horse may be treated then and there or the therapist will come up with a series of exercises for you to follow. It may sound obvious, but once you have been advised on a particular course of action, do not become fainthearted and stop too soon. A large percentage of owners do, and, not surprisingly, the problem persists. However, there is obviously no guarantee that even if you do follow the instructions to the letter, your horse will return to normal.

Monty Roberts and Joined-up Thinking

One man more than any other has had a major influence internationally on our understanding of horse behavior, as well as aspects of equine communication. Monty Roberts worked for many years as a rodeo rider and was therefore faced regularly with particularly difficult rides throughout his career. This led him to investigate the possibility of using the horse's natural behavior as a means of allowing him to communicate with his mount, and ultimately resulted in the development of what has since become known as the join-up technique. This technique places the rider firmly in control, as the dominant partner in the relationship, with the horse gradually learning to appreciate the benefit of co-operating with its rider. The method relies heavily on the rider's keen observation of the horse's body language, and a high level of confidence on the part of the rider concerned.

Although Monty Roberts has achieved remarkable results at public demonstrations, often "starting" a horse in under 30 minutes, join-up almost always requires longer to achieve permanent results. It has proved to be especially valuable to use with difficult horses, as well as those being started for riding.

glossary

Action The movement of the horse. The action in some cases may be characteristic of the breed, as for example in the Orlov trotter.

Aids Ways in which a rider can communicate with a horse, which includes the use of certain *tack*.

Backing This describes the process of teaching a young horse to accept a rider. It involves getting the youngster accustomed to the *tack* and to reacting to the *aids*.

Bars These are toothless areas in the horse's mouth, between the *incisors* at the front and the *molars* at the back. The *bit* rests on the bars of the lower jaw when it is fitted correctly.

Bit The metal, rubber, or plastic device on the bridle. This fits into the horse's mouth, over the tongue, and is used as a method of control during riding.

Blacksmith A qualified professional who works with horses' feet, keeping them trimmed and shod.

Breed A group of horses with distinctive, recognizable standard characteristics that will emerge in their offspring, leading to the description "pure-bred."

Cast When a horse is cast in its stable, it has slipped over, or laid down, and cannot get up. Cast horses can do themselves a lot of damage, and may be dangerous to try to help because they tend to thrash their legs about in an attempt to get up. When a shoe is cast, it has come off accidentally, rather than by the actions of the *blacksmith*.

Concentrates Formulated foodstuffs that help provide much of the horse's nutritional requirements in a concentrated form.

Conformation The overall appearance of the horse, based on its relative proportions. These will differ, depending on the *breed*, but individuals may also display poor conformation, which will affect their ability to work.

Cover The mating of a filly or a mare by a *stallion*, usually arranged where the stallion is being kept.

Crib biting A vice that results in a horse biting its stable door, or a fence rail outdoors. It may lead on to *wind sucking* if not corrected.

Dish face This is a feature particularly associated with Arab horses, which are known for their concave profile. It is a characteristic that they may pass on to halfbred offspring.

Dishing A fault in which the horse throws either one or both front legs outward in a circle as it moves forward.

Draft horse A heavy horse used for pulling carts or other loads rather than for riding purposes.

Feral horses Horses and their descendants that have reverted to living wild after having originally been domesticated.

Flehmening This describes the way that stallions curl their upper lips to sniff the air when a mare is coming into season. When they do this, the scent molecules are registering via Jacobsen's organ in the roof of the mouth.

Gait The way in which a horse moves, as well as the sequence of the movement of the feet. The common gaits are the walk, trot, canter, and gallop, but others are recognized as well.

Hack To ride out of the yard to exercise the horse and for the enjoyment of the rider, as opposed to schooling, which is usually done in a manège.

Hand The traditional method of measuring a horse, which is taken at the withers. One hand corresponds to 4in (10cm), the width of a human hand. For example, 14.3hh describes a horse that is 59 inches (150cm) high (14 x 4 + 3) at the withers; "hh" means "hands high."

Incisors The teeth at the front of the horse's mouth, used primarily for plucking herbage and grooming.

Lungeing Exercising in a school or paddock, with the horse moving in a circle around the handler. Aside from the long rein, the handler may also have a lungeing whip.

Molars The teeth at the rear of the mouth that are used for grinding up food before it is swallowed.

Nappy A horse that objects to going in the direction required, sometimes rearing or spinning around when obliged to do so.

Numnah The cloth that fits under the saddle to increase the horse's comfort and keep the underside of the saddle clean. It may be padded to reduce rubbing, although a well-fitted saddle should not require a numnah.

Pony A group of horses mainly distinguished by the fact that they measure less than 14.2hh when fully grown. They also have a relatively distinctive *conformation*.

Stallion An adult male horse that has not been castrated. Usually hard to manage, stallions are normally kept only for breeding purposes.

Strike off This refers to the first step of canter, i.e., the horse strikes off on the farside foot when cantering on a right lead.

Tack The equipment that is necessary for riding a horse, such as the saddle and bridle.

Twitch A loop of cord attached to a stick and used to restrain a horse. The loop fits over the muzzle and causes the release of endorphins, which seem to relax the horse.

Vice A behavioral problem that can range from a minor individual quirk to a serious flaw that can make the horse difficult to manage or ride.

Wind sucking This is when the horse stands and sucks air directly into its lungs. It is often linked with *crib biting*.

Wolf teeth The name given to small premolar teeth in the upper jaw. They are not always present, but will need to be removed to prevent difficulty in fitting a bit into the horse's mouth.

useful **addresses**

Affiliated National Riding Commission,
1900 Association Dr., Reston, VA 20191. Tel: 703-476-3450.
Fax: 800-886-0591. web address: www.anrc.org

American Association for Horsemanship Safety, Inc.,
P.O. Drawer 39, Fentress, TX 78622-0039. Tel: 512-488-2220.
Fax: 512-488-2319. email: jzdawson@aol.com

American Farrier's Association,
4059 Iron Works Pkwy., Ste. 2, Lexington, KY 40511-8434.
Tel: 859-233-7411. Fax: 859-231-7862. email:
info@americanfarriers.org

American Veterinary Medical Association,
1931 N. Meacham Rd., #100, Schaumburg, IL 60173-4360.
Tel: 800-248-2862 or in Washington D.C. 202-789-0007.
Fax: 847-925-1329.

North American Horsemen's Association,
310 Washburne Ave., Paynesville, MN 56362. Tel:
612-243-7250. Fax: 612-243-7224. email: ark@lkdllink.net

North American Riding for the Handicapped Association,
P.O. Box 33150, Denver, CO 80233. Tel: 303-452-1212 or
800-369-RIDE. Fax: 303-252-4610. web address:
www.narha.org

Saddle, Harness & Allied Trades Association,
1101-A Broad St., Oriental, NC 28571. Tel: 252-249-3414.
Fax: 252-249-3409.

United States Pony Clubs, Inc.,
4071 Iron Works Pkwy., Lexington, KY 40511-8462.
Tel: 859-254-PONY (7669). Fax: 859-233-4652. email:
uspc@ponyclub.org

AHC State and Local Member Organizations

Arizona Thoroughbred Breeders' Association, Inc.,
P.O. Box 41774, Phoenix, AZ 85080-1774. Tel: 602-942-1310.
Fax: 602-942-8225. email: atba@worldnet.att.net

California Harness Horsemen's Association, Inc.,
P.O. Box 254767, Sacramento, CA 95865-4767.
Tel: 916-263-7888. Fax: 916-263-7887.

California Thoroughbred Breeders' Association,
P.O. Box 60018, Arcadia, CA 91066-6018. Tel: 626-445-7800.
Fax: 626-574-0852. email: info@ctba.com

Delaware Thoroughbred Horsemen's Association, Inc.,
777 Delaware Park Blvd., Wilmington, DE 19804-4122.
Tel: 302-994-2521, x284. Fax: 302-994-3392. email:
DTHAinc@aol.com

Empire State Quarter Horse Association,
4530 New Rd., Williamson, NY 14589. Tel: 315-589-2335.
email: esqha@hotmail.com

Florida Thoroughbred Breeders' & Owners' Association,
801 SW 60th Ave., Ocala, FL 34474-1827. Tel: 352-629-2160.
Fax: 352-629-3603. email: FTBOA@aol.com

Illinois Thoroughbred Horsemen's Association,
P.O. Box 50366, Cicero, IL 60650. Tel: 708-652-2201.
Fax: 708-652-2259.

Kentucky Thoroughbred Association, Inc.,
4079 Iron Works Pkwy., Lexington, KY 40511-8483.
Tel: 859-381-1414. Fax: 859-233-9737. email:
contact@kta-ktob.com

Louisiana Thoroughbred Breeders' Association,
P.O. Box 24650, New Orleans, LA 70184. Tel: 504-947-4676.
Fax: 504-943-2149. email: ltba@iamerica.net

Maryland Horse Breeders Association, Inc.,
P.O. Box 427, Timonium, MD 21094-0427. Tel: 410-252-2100.
Fax: 410-560-0503. web address: www.mdhorsebreeders.com

Maryland Thoroughbred Horsemen's Association, Inc.,
6314 Windsor Mill Rd., Baltimore, MD 21207-6088.
Tel: 410-265-6842. Fax: 410-265-6841. email:
mdhorsemen@erols.com

Michigan Harness Horsemen's Association,
4650 Moore St., P.O. Box 349, Okemos, MI 48805.
Tel: 517-349-2920. Fax: 517-349-4983. email:
lmallar@voyager.net

Minnesota Thoroughbred Association,
P.O. Box 508, Shakopee, MN 55379-0508. Tel: 952-496-3770.
Fax: 952-496-3672. email: mtassoc@voyager.net

New York Thoroughbred Breeders, Inc.,
57 Philadelphia St., Saratoga Springs, NY 12866-3110.
Tel: 518-587-0777. Fax: 518-587-1551. email:
thoroughbred@acmenet.net

New York Thoroughbred Horsemen's Association,
P.O. Box 170070, Jamaica, NY 11417-9981. Tel:
718-848-5045-Aqueduct; 516-488-2337-Belmont. Fax:
718-848-9269-Aqueduct; 516-488-1698-Belmont.

Oklahoma Quarter Horse Association,
P.O. Box 991, Edmond, OK 73083. Tel: 405-348-1035.
Fax: 405-348-1043.

Palm Beach Equestrian Commission, Inc,
222 Lakeview Ave., Ste. 1200, West Palm Beach, FL 33401.
Tel: 561-793-6461. Fax: 561-333-8484.

South Carolina Department of Agriculture,
P.O. Box 11280, Columbia, SC 29211-1280. Tel: 803-734-2200.
Fax: 803-734-0325. email: Kay@SCDA.STATE.SC.US

Standardbred Breeders & Owners Association of New Jersey,
P.O. Box 839, Freehold, NJ 07728-0839. Tel: 732-462-2357.
Fax: 732-409-0741.

Tennessee Department of Agriculture Marketing Division,
P.O. Box 40627, Nashville, TN 37204-0627. Tel: 615-837-5160.
Fax: 615-837-5194. email: mmbaker@mail.state.tn.us

Texas Quarter Horse Association,
P.O. Box 16229, Austin, TX 78761. Tel: 512-458-5202.
Fax: 512-458-1713.

Texas Thoroughbred Association,
P.O. Box 14967, Austin, TX 78761-4967. Tel: 512-458-6133.
Fax: 512-453-5919. email: davidh@texasthoroughbred.com

Thoroughbred Owners of California,
285 W. Huntington Dr., Arcadia, CA 91007. Tel: 626-574-6620
or 800-994-9909. Fax: 626-821-1515.

Virginia Thoroughbred Association,
38 Garrett St., Warrenton, VA 20186-3107. Tel: 540-347-4313.
Fax: 540-347-7314. web address: www.vabred.org

Washington Thoroughbred Breeders' Association, Inc.,
P.O. Box 1499, Auburn, WA 98071-1499. Tel: 253-288-7878. Fax:
253-288-7890. email: maindesk@washingtonthoroughbred.com

index